WILLS FOR ALBERTA

Cheryl C. Gottselig, Q.C.

Self-Counsel Press
(a division of)
International Self-Counsel Press Ltd.
Canada U.S.A.

Printed in Canada.

First edition: 1974
Tenth edition: 1994; Reprinted: 1995
Eleventh edition: 1997
Twelfth edition: 1998; Reprinted: 2000

Canadian Cataloguing in Publication Data
Gottselig, Cheryl.
    Wills for Alberta

    (Self-counsel legal series)
    ISBN 1-55180-211-2

    1. Wills — Alberta — Popular works. 2. Probate law and practice — Alberta — Popular works. I. Title. II. Series.

KEA245.Z82G68 1997   346.712305'4   C97-910162-X
KF755.Z9G68 1997

Self-Counsel Press
(a division of)
International Self-Counsel Press Ltd.

1481 Charlotte Road   1704 N. State Street
North Vancouver, BC V7J lHl   Bellingham, WA 98225
          Canada   U.S.A.

CONTENTS

PREFACE   xi

1 WILLS AND YOUR LAWYER   1

   a. What is a will?   1

   b. When does a will take effect?   1

   c. What is a holograph will?   2

   d. Who needs a lawyer?   2

   e. Legal fees   3

   f. Should everyone have a will?   3

   g. What happens if you die without a will?   4

2 DRAFTING YOUR OWN WILL   6

   a. Essentials of a will   6

      1. Format   6

      2. Signing and witnessing the will   11

      3. Testamentary capacity   12

      4. Undue influence   13

      5. Age   14

      6. Domicile   14

   b. How to appoint a personal representative   14

   c. The common disaster clause   15

   d. Specific bequests   17

   e. Special clauses   19

      1. Life estate   19

      2. Gifts to infants   25

      3. Investments   26

      4. Co-personal representatives   30

	5.	A guardian	30
	6.	Funeral instructions	32
	7.	Body donation	33
	8.	Organ transplants	33
	9.	Eye bank	33
	10.	Charity	34
	11.	RRSPs	35
	12.	Accounts receivable	35
	13.	Use of a memorandum	36
f.		What about debts?	36
g.		Can you disinherit a dependant?	37
h.		How to make changes in a will	39
i.		How often should a will be revised?	42
j.		How to revoke a will	43
k.		Marriage and wills	43
l.		What happens if you move to another province?	45
m.		Personal Directives Act	46
	1.	What is a personal directive?	47
	2.	Who is an agent?	48
	3.	When does a personal directive come into effect?	48
	4.	What form should a personal directive take?	49
n.		Problems	54
o.		Summary of steps in the execution of a will	54
p.		Enduring powers of attorney	56
3		**PROBATE**	61
a.		What is probate?	61
b.		What are the duties of a personal representative?	62
c.		Checklist for the personal representative	62

d.	What happens to jointly owned property?	65
e.	Which judicial district do you apply in?	66
f.	What about a bond?	67
g.	Lack of sufficient funds in the estate	67
h.	The time period for distribution	68
i.	Fees of personal representatives	69
j.	Fees of lawyers	69
k.	Readily available money	71
l.	Foreign death duties	73
4	**ADMINISTRATION**	**98**
a.	What is an administrator?	98
b.	Administration with will annexed	99
c.	What is a public trustee?	105
d.	Common-law marriages and administration	105
	1. Income Tax Act	108
	2. Canada Pension Plan	108
	3. Family Relief Act	108
	4. Matrimonial Property Act	109
	5. Interstate Succession Act	109
	6. Dower Act	109
	7. Domestic Relations Act	109
	8. Unjust enrichment	110
e.	How is the estate divided if there is no will?	111
f.	Examples of administration	112
5	**TAX CONSIDERATIONS**	**114**
a.	Capital gains tax	114
b.	Capital gains on death	114
c.	Filing the tax return	115

d.	Tax clearance certificate	116
e.	What impact the GST has on estates	116
6	**THE CANADA PENSION PLAN**	**118**
a.	Benefits under the plan	118
b.	Lump-sum death benefit	119
c.	Survivors' pension	120
d.	Benefits for dependent children	121
e.	Common-law relationships	122
	GLOSSARY	**129**

TABLES

#1	Suggested fee guidelines for personal representatives	70
#2	Fee guidelines for lawyers	71
#3	Property type and GST consequences	117

SAMPLES

#1	Master will	7
#2	Basic will	20
#3	Will for a married person leaving entire estate absolutely to spouse and adult children	21
#4	Will of a single person in favor of parents for life and then equally to brothers and sisters absolutely	23
#5	Will with a trust arrangement for infant children	27
#6	A codicil	40
#7	Codicil revoking will	44

#8	Will made in contemplation of marriage	45
#9	Personal directive	50
#10	Enduring power of attorney	57
#11	Application by a personal representative for a grant of probate — Form NC1	75
#12	Affidavit by a personal representative on application for a grant of probate — Form NC2	77
#13	Schedule 1: Particulars of deceased — Form NC3	79
#14	Schedule 2: Will — Form NC4	81
#15	Affidavit of witness to a will — Form NC8	82
#16	Schedule 3: Particulars of the personal representative(s) — Form NC5	83
#17	Schedule 4: Particulars of beneficiaries — Form NC6	84
#18	Schedule 5: Inventory of property and debts — Form NC7	86
#19	Notice to beneficiaries (residuary) —Form NC19	89
#20	Affidavit of service — Form NC27	90
#21	Transfer of land	92
#22	Application for transmission	97
#23	Division of an estate	100
#24	Application for grant of administration — Form NC1	101
#25	Affidavit by personal representative on application for grant of administration	103
#26	Application for grant of administration with will annexed — Form NC1	106
#27	Application for death benefits	123
#28	Application for survivors' benefits	124
#29	Declaration of attendance at school or university	126
#30	Application for child's benefit	127

NOTICE TO READERS

Laws are constantly changing. Every effort is made to keep this publication as current as possible. However, the author, the publisher, and the vendor of this book make no representation or warranties regarding the outcome or the use to which the information in this book is put and are not assuming any liability for any claims, losses, or damages arising out of the use of this book. The reader should not rely on the author or the publisher of this book for any professional advice. Please be sure that you have the most recent edition.

Note: The fees quoted in this book are correct at the date of publication. However, fees are subject to change without notice. For current fees, please check with the court registry or appropriate government office nearest you.

AVAILABLE FROM THE PUBLISHER

Have You Made Your Will?

If you wish to make your own will, Self-Counsel Press sells a will and estate planning kit, entitled *Have You Made Your Will?*, that will help you do it yourself. The kit includes enough forms for two people to make their own wills:

> 2 blank will forms for each person
>
> 1 estate and business planning guide
>
> 1 checklist of things to do when a death occurs
>
> 2 living will forms

Available as a forms-only package for $6.95, **Have You Made Your Will?** is also available on computer disk for $11.95, allowing you to fill out and print your will on your PC.

ORDER FORM

To: Self-Counsel Press
        1481 Charlotte Road
        North Vancouver, BC V7J 1H1

Please send me:

_____Have You Made Your Will?, $6.95

_____Have You Made Your Will? (with disk), $11.95

Please add $3.00 postage to your order and GST to the total.

All prices subject to change without notice.

❑ Money order enclosed for $_____.

❑ Charge to my credit card (see below).

Name_____

Address _____

City _____ Province _____

Postal Code _____Telephone_____

MasterCard/Visa number:_____

Expiry date:_____ Validation date: _____

Signature:_____

PREFACE

Even though the preparation of a will may conjure up morbid thoughts of death and funerals, it is a topic everyone should consider carefully in the early years of their lives. The failure to do this all-important task has resulted in innumerable family-splitting disputes and lawsuits. The way in which you choose to distribute your goods may not always please your beneficiaries, but at least if you make the decision there will be less likelihood of quarrels erupting. Therefore, to insure the well-being of your immediate family and friends in the event of an unexpected tragedy, you should make a will.

When preparing your will you must be aware of the document's legal aspects. After all, if your will does not meet the legal requirements of the province you live in, it will not be worth the paper it is written on.

The purpose of this book is to set out the considerations that must be kept in mind when you or your lawyer are making a will.

There are many things to consider when preparing a very simple will, most of which are generally unknown. In a short discussion such as this, one cannot hope to examine thoroughly all the problems and rules relating to the preparation of a will. However, the book will touch on the major topics to give you a general idea of the situation. It will also illustrate the problems that can arise if there is no will and point out the many reasons why a will is a necessity. If, in the end, you go to a lawyer, your knowledge will save time and expense as you will have a much clearer idea of what it is all about than if you had not read the book.

1
WILLS AND YOUR LAWYER

a. WHAT IS A WILL?

Webster's New World Dictionary defines a will as the legal statement of a person's wishes concerning the disposal of his or her property after death. In this document, the person making the will, called the "testator" (or "testatrix" if a woman), appoints a person called a "personal representative" who is empowered to carry out the instructions set out in the will.

The powers of a personal representative include the right to collect assets, discharge any outstanding debts, and divide the remainder of your property according to the directions left in the will. A testator may also appoint guardians for his or her children and direct how he or she is to be buried.

b. WHEN DOES A WILL TAKE EFFECT?

By signing a will, you do not in any way restrict the disposal of your assets during the rest of your life. In other words, a will is said to "speak" only at the moment of death.

For example, even if you have signed a will leaving your home to your brother, you are perfectly free to sell your home the next day without the consent of your brother. Upon your death, the will is read as though no gift of the house was contained in it. In short, a person to whom a specific asset was left (called the "beneficiary") gets nothing if the asset has already been disposed of.

c. WHAT IS A HOLOGRAPH WILL?

A will written entirely in the testator's own handwriting is called a "holograph will." Valid holograph wills have appeared in many unusual forms. For example, a farmer who has written on his tractor fender, "In case I, George Farmer, die in this mess, I leave all to my wife," has made a proper holograph will.

The advantages of the holograph will are that no witnesses are required so it can be drawn by someone near death who is alone, and it enables those unaware of formal legal stipulations to make a valid will.

A holograph will must be written *entirely* in the testator's own handwriting. A common mistake is that the testator will use a pre-printed will form, fill in the blanks in his or her own handwriting, and sign it. This is not a holograph will, because he or she did not write it in full. A pre-printed will form also requires two witnesses. (For more about who may witness a will, see chapter 2.)

The advantages of making a holograph will, however, are usually offset by the tendency of people to scribble a will carelessly without taking care to precisely express their wishes.

Holograph wills are valid for residents of Alberta, Ontario, Manitoba, and Saskatchewan, but not for residents of British Columbia.

d. WHO NEEDS A LAWYER?

In most cases, a valid will can be drafted without the assistance of a lawyer. However, the following categories of people should always consult a lawyer:

(a) Owners of large, complex estates would be wise to seek legal advice on how to distribute their assets to obtain the greatest tax benefits. The time and money spent in estate planning is generally a small investment which returns considerable peace of mind during your life and tax benefits when death occurs.

(b) People who are separated or contemplating divorce should make adequate provisions to prevent the estranged spouse from inheriting their entire estate.

(c) Older people who may be subject to undue influence from younger members of their family should seek the independent advice of a good lawyer.

(d) People contemplating marriage should have the advice of a lawyer.

e. LEGAL FEES

As our society becomes more sophisticated and more complicated, it is a natural progression that wills become more complex, and in more and more situations professional advice and guidance is required.

While there is no set price among lawyers for the preparation of a will, a simple will involving no tax planning will probably cost somewhere between $150 and $250. Do not rely entirely on these figures because if there are complications, the fee will be considerably higher. The best advice is to ask the lawyer in advance what the fee will be.

A lawyer may quote a set fee or, if the situation is more complicated, charge an hourly rate ranging from $50 to $300 per hour depending on the problem and the expertise required to solve it. Though these sums may appear high, if large estates are involved or complex tax problems have to be faced, it will be well worth the cost.

f. SHOULD EVERYONE HAVE A WILL?

The simple answer to this question is yes. A will is important for a variety of reasons. When an individual dies "intestate," that is, without a will, the administration of his or her estate may be complicated by lengthy court procedures before the assets can be distributed to the heirs-at-law.

More important, the assets of the dead person may pass to heirs whom he or she did not wish to benefit if no will directs how such assets are to be distributed. Conversely, relatives and heirs whom the deceased would have wanted to benefit and whom he or she believed would inherit the estate may receive less than the deceased intended or nothing at all.

The prime example of this is the common misconception that when a married man dies without a will the whole of his property passes to the surviving wife. This is not the case. Depending on whether or not there are children of the marriage, the surviving wife may end up with less than two-thirds of her deceased husband's estate.

The value of having a will cannot be over-emphasized, regardless of the size of the estate involved. In order to simplify matters upon your death and to ensure that your property passes to those whom you want to benefit, a will is essential.

g. WHAT HAPPENS IF YOU DIE WITHOUT A WILL?

Two problems arise in administering the estate of a person who dies intestate. First, no one will have been appointed by the deceased to act as a personal representative of the estate. Second, the deceased person will not have indicated in a legal form how he or she wishes property to be distributed. In that case, the Alberta law that provides for each of these eventualities will come into effect.

The Intestate Succession Act provides for the appointment of an "administrator" (or "administratrix" if a woman) to act as personal representative to distribute the estate of a person who dies without a will (subject to variation by a court order under the Family Relief Act and the Matrimonial Property Act.) The functions of an administrator are basically the same as those of a personal representative named under a will. The Intestate Succession Act also provides for the distribution of property to the blood relatives of a person dying without a will. (See Sample #20 in chapter 4 for a breakdown of who gets what.)

If there is no will and the deceased has no spouse or blood relative, all his or her property will pass to the provincial government pursuant to the Ultimate Heir Act. In legal terminology the property "escheats" to the Crown.

2

DRAFTING YOUR OWN WILL

a. ESSENTIALS OF A WILL

You should always exercise caution in preparing your will as it is a very important document. If it is improperly prepared and the error is only discovered after death, then it is too late. Your wishes will be ignored because the estate will be disposed of under the Intestate Succession Act as though you had died without a will.

If you intend to prepare your will by using the publisher's will and estate planning kit or software package described at the beginning of this book or by starting from scratch, be certain that you have read through this chapter very carefully before beginning. Should you desire anything but the simplest of wills you would be well advised to consult a lawyer. The charge for preparing your will is small in comparison with the peace of mind you get from knowing that your estate will be distributed according to your wishes.

Sample #1 shows a master will which indicates which matters are often addressed in a typical will.

1. Format

A will does not have to follow any special form. You need not use any special legal words. It is only necessary that the will clearly state your intentions. Lawyers usually follow standard forms (see Samples #1 through #5) only because over the years these forms have proven to be the most satisfactory. The will need not be typewritten but may be in your own handwriting or the handwriting of any other person.

6

SAMPLE #1
MASTER WILL

Preamble Clause — Name and address of testator

"THIS IS THE LAST WILL AND TESTAMENT of me, Annie Be-good, of the City of Medicine Hat, in the Province of Alberta."

1. Revocation of earlier wills

"I REVOKE all former wills and codicils."

2. Appointment of personal representatives

"I APPOINT Ernie Executor to be the personal representative of my will."

3. Provision for substitute personal representatives

"But if my said personal representative should refuse to act, prede-cease me, or die within a period of 30 days following my decease, or without having proved this my will, then I appoint Thomas Terrific to be the personal representative of my will."

4. Funeral wishes

"I DIRECT my remains to be cremated."

or

"I DIRECT THAT I be buried in a simple manner and that all expenses in connection with my burial be kept to a bare minimum."

5. Declaration as to testator's domicile if considered necessary

"I DECLARE THAT I was born in London, England where I was raised and educated and England was my domicile of origin. In 1984 I came to Canada where I resided in Toronto and attended university. In 1990 I took up residence in Medicine Hat where I have been employed ever since. I have married and consider my domi-cile of choice to be Alberta."

6. Appointment of guardian of infant children, effective on death of surviving spouse

"IF MY HUSBAND shall predecease me, then on my death I appoint John Begood to be the guardian of my infant children."

7. Realization clause — Payment of debts, funeral expenses, etc.

"I DIRECT my personal representative to pay my just debts, funeral and testamentary expenses, and all income taxes, estate, inheritance, and succession duties or taxes wheresoever payable."

8. Bequest of personal articles

"I DIRECT my personal representative to transfer and deliver absolutely my diamond ring to my daughter, Sally Begood."

9. Cash legacies

"I DIRECT my personal representative to pay the following cash legacies as soon after my death as practicable to such of the following named legatees as are alive at my death:

(a) $1 000 to my mother, Anne Brown;

(b) $500 to my friend, Mabel Moses."

10. Bequest of everything to personal representative to deal with according to specific instructions

"I GIVE all of the residue of my property of every nature and kind and wherever situated to my personal representative upon the following trusts:

(a) In the event that my said husband, Sam Begood, survives me for a period of 30 days, I direct my personal representative to pay or transfer to my said husband the residue of my estate for his own use absolutely;

(b) In the event that my said husband shall predecease me or, surviving me, dies within a period of 30 days following my decease, I direct my personal representative to divide the residue of my estate equally among my three children, Sally Begood and James Begood and Jack Begood, for their own use absolutely; provided that if any of my said children predecease me, then the issue of such deceased child, if any, shall be entitled to the share of their deceased parent, such share to be divided among such issue in equal shares per stirpes.* If there is no issue of such deceased child of mine, then the

*Note: See Glossary for definition of "per stirpes."

share of such child shall be divided among such of my issue as may be alive at my death in equal shares per stirpes."

11. Distribution of residue of estate

"I DIRECT my personal representative to invest the residue of my estate upon the following trusts:

(a) Wide investment clause

"Unless provided otherwise, to invest and keep invested the residue of my estate; and I declare that my personal representative, when making investments for my estate, shall not be limited to investments authorized by law but may make any investments which, in his uncontrolled discretion, he considers advisable."

or

(a) Limited investment clause

"To invest, and reinvest, assets of my estate in any investments from time to time allowed by law in the Province of Alberta for the investment of trust funds."

and

(b) Where infant children are involved

"To hold and keep invested the residue of my estate in trust and the income and capital or so much thereof as my personal representative in his absolute discretion deems advisable shall be used for the benefit, maintenance and education of my children then alive until the youngest shall reach the age of 18 at which time my personal representative shall divide the residue of my estate then remaining in equal shares among my children then alive."

or

"As each child attains the age of 18 years the remainder of each child's share shall be paid to such child for his or her own use absolutely."

or, if there are no children

"To pay or transfer the residue of my estate to my said husband if he survives me for a period of 30 days, for his own use absolutely."

IN WITNESS WHEREOF, I have hereunto set my hand this 3rd day of May, 200-.

SIGNED, PUBLISHED, AND DECLARED by the said Testatrix, Annie Begood, as and for her last will and testament, in the presence of us, both present at the same time, who at her request, in her presence and in the presence of each other, have hereunto subscribed our names as witnesses.

Annie Begood
(Testatrix signs here)

Uma Witness
(Witness sign)

101 Self-Counsel Way, Medicine Hat
Address

Clerk
Occupation

UMA WITNESS
(Witness sign)

305 Probate Lane, Medicine Hat
Address

Saleswoman
Occupation

A will generally starts out by identifying the person making it and by disclosing his or her residence and occupation. This is usually done by words such as the following:

> This is the last will and testament of me, Tammy Testator, currently residing at 111 Principle Street in the City of Calgary, in the Province of Alberta.

The first clause of the will should state that all previous wills are revoked. If you make more than one will during your lifetime, the will bearing the latest date governs. It is, however, always advisable to expressly revoke earlier wills in order to avoid any confusion or questions at the time of death. A simple revocation clause is as follows:

> I revoke all former wills and codicils.

2. Signing and witnessing the will

In order to be valid, all wills (except holograph wills, of course) must be witnessed by two people who actually saw you sign the will. There is no rule that witnesses must be of any certain age. However, it is wise to have witnesses who are old enough to know what is going on so that they can confirm that the will was properly signed when it is probated after death. Your signature should come on the last page of the will, after all the provisions you wish to make have been set out.

The two witnesses watch you sign the will and watch each other sign in the spaces provided. If it later comes to light that the witnessing of the will was not properly carried out, the will is declared invalid.

A very important limitation on who is able to be a witness to a will should be noted at this point. Any person who is to receive a benefit under the will, that is, any beneficiary, must not be a witness to the will. Likewise, neither the husband nor the wife of any beneficiary under the will should be a witness.

If this rule is broken, the will is not invalidated, but the gift to the beneficiary who acted as a witness or to the beneficiary whose spouse acted as a witness will not be effective. The will shall be read as though no such gift were contained in it, and the part of the estate that would have gone to such beneficiary will now pass to the residuary beneficiary, that is, the person to whom the remainder or the residue of the estate is left. Though the will remains valid, the intentions of the person making the will may be thwarted due to a lack of attention to this rule.

If the will is contained on more than one page of paper, it is a good idea for you and your witnesses to place your initials in the lower right-hand corner of each of the pages, with the exception of the final page upon which the signatures appear. This is not a legal requirement, but it prevents any person from substituting some of the earlier pages of the will at a later date. It would be easy to carry out the substitution if it were not necessary to forge initials.

If the will contains any corrections, insertions, or deletions, you and your witnesses should initial them before the will is signed at the end.

If this is not done, when the will is submitted to the court it will be necessary to convince the judge that the will has not been tampered with and that the changes were made before it was signed. The better procedure is to re-type or rewrite any page with corrections prior to signing the will.

3. Testamentary capacity

You must have what is called "testamentary capacity" when your will is made. It must be clear on the facts that you were of sound mind, memory, and understanding when the will was signed. While a will made when you have full capacity does not become invalid if you later become insane, your capacity at the time the will was signed is important to the validity of the will. Testamentary capacity involves three criteria:

(a) You must understand that you are giving property away as of the date of death.

(b) You must be aware of the nature and extent of your property.

(c) You must be aware of the various claims upon your property which your dependants may have.

Lack of testamentary capacity at the date of signing the will is not fatal provided that —

(a) you had capacity when you gave instructions,

(b) the will was prepared strictly following those instructions, and

(c) you understood you were signing a will prepared according to your instructions.

4. Undue influence

Fraud and undue influence are not really questions of testamentary capacity because it is not your capacity that is the problem but whether the acts of others have induced you to make dispositions that you did not really want to make. Questions of undue influence most commonly arise with people of weak mental capacity or failing health.

The undue influence that will set aside a will must amount to force or coercion. The onus of proving undue influence lies on those attacking the will. A number of things must be proven before a court will set aside a will due to undue influence:

(a) Motive

(b) Opportunity to exercise influence

(c) Positive proof of coercion overpowering the wishes of the person making the will

The fact that a person had motive and opportunity and benefited under the will is not sufficient to prove undue influence.

5. Age

In Alberta you must be 18 years old to draw up a valid will unless you are married, a mariner or seaman, or a member of the Canadian Armed Forces. If you are in one of these categories of people, you can make a valid will even if you are not 18.

6. Domicile

In most cases, it is advisable to insert a declaration of domicile in the will. This is simply a declaration by you stating where you consider your home to be. If you have assets outside Alberta, a lawyer should be consulted because those assets could be governed by the law of another jurisdiction.

b. HOW TO APPOINT A PERSONAL REPRESENTATIVE

No magic words are required to appoint a personal representative in a will. Any words that clearly indicate that the person you name is to carry out the provisions of your will will be effective to make that person a personal representative. However, it is always advisable to state specifically that the person named is to be the personal representative of the will. This prevents any doubts arising as to your intentions. Your will should be as clear as possible as you will not be around to consult when it is finally put to use.

The following is an example of a clause that should be inserted to appoint a personal representative:

> I appoint my wife, Willa Vie, to be the personal representative of my will if she survives me.

If an alternate personal representative is desired, the following words should be added to the above appointment:

> If my said wife predeceases me or refuses to act as personal representative of my will, I nominate and appoint my lawyer, Gordon Goodbody, to be the personal representative of my will.

Personal representatives may act either jointly or alone. They are usually chosen from one of the following groups:

(a) Relatives or close friends

(b) Business associates

(c) Trust companies

You should select a person who is your own age or younger to be your personal representative. There is little point in selecting someone 20 years older as that person will probably die before you do, so the appointment will be worthless.

Your personal representative should be a mature person with some knowledge of business matters. He or she should be trustworthy and capable of making reasoned decisions. It also helps if your spouse approves of your choice. Your personal representative should reside in Alberta as administrative difficulties could arise if, for example, assets of the estate and the personal representative are located in different provinces.

Furthermore, if a personal representative is not an Alberta resident, the court will probably require a bond to be posted. (This is like an insurance policy, which assures the court that the estate will be properly distributed.) Your personal representative should be 18 years of age or older. You are always wise to appoint an alternate personal representative in case the first person you select is unable or unwilling to act.

c. THE COMMON DISASTER CLAUSE

Most wills include a common disaster provision. The following example shows why this is important. Assume that a young married couple have each made a will in which all the assets of the one are left to the surviving spouse in the event of death. Assume also that the husband and the wife are both killed in a car accident and die instantly. Let us assume that, as is often the case, the wife is younger than the husband. Under Alberta law, if two people die at the same time or in circumstances where it is impossible to know which died first, it is presumed that the older of the two people died first.

The husband's will provided that all his property should go to his wife in the event of his death. The wife's will provided that all her property should go to the husband in the event of her death. It also went on to provide that if her husband happened to die before she did, then her property was to go to her mother.

Given the above facts, and bearing in mind the law which assumes that the wife outlived the husband, all the assets of the husband pass to the wife and form part of her estate. Almost immediately thereafter, the wife is assumed to have died and all her assets pass to her mother.

The effect is that the husband's assets must first be administered as part of a separate and distinct estate before they are included in the wife's estate that eventually passes to her mother. Also, where the marriage was short, there is often a great deal of unnecessary animosity between surviving parents.

To avoid these difficulties, you should insert a common disaster provision, or a "30-day clause" as it is sometimes called. For example, instead of leaving all of the assets to the wife, the husband's will should provide as follows:

> I give all of my property of every nature and kind and wheresoever situate to my wife, Mary May, provided that she survives me for a period of 30 days. If she fails to survive me for 30 days then all of my property to my brother, Marvin May.

If Mary May does not outlive her husband by 30 days, she is not eligible to receive the gift contained in the will. Assuming that the husband's will contained an alternate gift to his brother in the event of his wife's death, his estate would pass to his brother even though the law presumes his wife survived him momentarily.

This sort of provision takes into account the possibility of a joint death or disaster and has the effect of avoiding the need to administer the husband's assets as part of two estates. The 30-day clause is especially important in the case where both spouses are leaving everything to each other with no alternate beneficiary. In the event of a joint disaster and *no* 30-day clause, the wills would have no effect and the estate would be distributed to the closest blood relatives of the younger spouse, through a long and costly process of the court called administration (to be discussed later).

Note that there is no special magic in the words "30 days"; you may insert whatever time limit you wish. This time limit is generally considered adequate to cover a genuine joint disaster situation while at the same time avoiding a lengthy delay in getting the estate probated.

d. SPECIFIC BEQUESTS

You may want to leave specific items or a fixed amount of money to a relative, friend, or charity. For instance, if you wish to leave your nephew, Don, a sum of money, words to the following effect would be inserted in your will:

> I give to my nephew, Don Doe, the sum of
> One Thousand Dollars ($1 000).

If a specific article is to be left to a named person, then the article in question should be described in sufficient detail in the will so that the personal representative will be able to identify it. For instance, if you wish to leave to your niece, Ann, a painting, words to the following effect should be inserted in your will:

> I give to my niece, Anne Arte, my painting
> entitled Autumn Leaves by Tom Thompson.

This detail would probably be sufficient to identify the painting you had in mind.

Generally, the specific bequest clauses follow those in which you revoke all earlier wills and appoint a personal representative.

You may want to provide for a few specific bequests of money or individual items and then go on to provide that the remainder or the "residue" of the estate be delivered over to another named person. Alternatively, the residue may be divided among a group of persons, identified either by name or by description (such as "my children").

If you act as a foster parent, or as a parent to someone who is not legally adopted, it is best to name the children, rather than let doubts arise about whom you actually meant to include in your reference to "children."

An example of a gift of the remainder or the residue of an estate is as follows:

> I direct my personal representative to pay or transfer all the rest and residue of my estate to my wife, Willa Vie, provided that she survives me for a period of 30 days.

An example of a gift of the residue to a group of persons might be as follows:

> I direct my personal representative to divide the rest and residue of my estate into as many equal shares as there shall be children of mine alive at the time of my death and to pay or transfer one of such equal shares to each of such children.

All wills should contain a clause disposing of the residue of the estate. Some people make extensive lists of specific bequests in which they give away all of their assets to relatives and friends by naming the particular asset to be left to a specific beneficiary. Then they feel that it is unnecessary to provide for a gift of the residue of their estate in the will. This is a mistake, since one or more of the named beneficiaries may die before they receive their gift. The gift would not be effective and the will gives no direction about what would happen to the asset in question. A residuary gift would prevent this situation from arising as the particular asset would fall into the residue of the estate and would go to the person who was to receive the residue of the estate as a gift.

The residuary gift also looks after the situation where a person acquires new and different assets after the will is made. Many people acquire assets of value after making their wills in spite of their belief that they are unlikely to do so.

Sample #2 shows a basic will. Sample #3 shows a will for a married person who wishes to leave everything to the spouse and adult children. Sample #4 shows a will for a single person who wishes to leave the estate to parents for life and then equally to brothers and sisters.

e. SPECIAL CLAUSES

There are an almost infinite variety of special clauses that you may include in your will beyond the normal provisions discussed above. This section of the chapter deals with some of the clauses you may wish to include in your will.

1. Life estate

Where you have accumulated a fairly large estate, you may provide for what is known as a "life estate" or a "life interest." By doing this, you are able to control an asset like land or money after your death.

The most common clause of this sort is one that permits a spouse to make use of a matrimonial home during the remainder of his or her lifetime and then directs that the home be given outright to a child or children on his or her death.

Another example is where one spouse leaves the other a life interest in a sum of money. The deceased's will provides that the survivor will receive a life interest in $100 000, for example. This means that the $100 000 is invested and the

SAMPLE #2
BASIC WILL

THIS IS THE LAST WILL AND TESTAMENT of me, Samuel Smarte, of the City of Calgary, in the Province of Alberta, truck driver.

1. I REVOKE all former wills and codicils.

2. I APPOINT my wife, Sarah Smarte, to be the personal representative of this my will.

3. I GIVE all my property of every nature and kind and wheresoever situate, including any property over which I may have a general power of appointment, to my said wife, Sarah Smarte, for her own use absolutely.

IN TESTIMONY WHEREOF I have to this my last will and testament written upon this single page of paper subscribed to my name this 10th day of April, 200-.

SIGNED, PUBLISHED, AND DECLARED by the said Testator, Samuel Smarte, as and for his last will and testament, in the presence of us, both present at the same time, who, at his request, in his presence and in the presence of each other, have hereunto subscribed our names as witnesses.

Samuel Smarte

(Testator signs here)

Ima Witness	UMA WITNESS
Witness	Witness
112 Western Road, Calgary	115 Eastern Lane, Calgary
Address	Address
Truck Driver	Salesperson
Occupation	Occupation

WILL FOR A MARRIED PERSON LEAVING ENTIRE ESTATE ABSOLUTELY TO SPOUSE AND ADULT CHILDREN*

THIS IS THE LAST WILL AND TESTAMENT of me, Thomas Terrific, of the City of Edmonton, in the Province of Alberta.

1. I REVOKE all former wills and codicils.

2. I APPOINT my wife to be the personal representative of this my will. In the event that she predeceases me, I appoint Terrence Terrific of the City of Calgary, in the Province of Alberta, to be the personal representative of this my will.

3. I DIRECT my personal representative to pay out of the capital of my estate my just debts, funeral, and testamentary expenses and all income taxes, estate, inheritance and succession duties or taxes wheresoever payable.

4. I GIVE the following legacies:

(a) If my wife survives me for a period of 30 days, I GIVE, DEVISE, AND BEQUEATH the residue of my real and personal property whatsoever and wheresoever situate, including any property over which I may have a general power of appointment, to my said wife.

(b) If, however, my wife predeceases me or fails to survive me for the said period of 30 days, then I GIVE all my real and personal property whatsoever and wheresoever situate, including any property over which I may have a general power of appointment, to my children namely: Tommy Terrific and Tammy Terrific to be divided equally between them but only if they survive me for a period of 30 days.

(c) If any of my said children shall predecease me, then the issue of such deceased child shall take equal shares per stirpes the share which the deceased child of mine would have been entitled to were he or she living at my death.

*Note: The same form may be used by a married woman in favor of her husband and children.

IN WITNESS WHEREOF I have hereunto set my hand this 5th day of June, 200-.

SIGNED, PUBLISHED, AND DECLARED by the said Testator, Thomas Terrific, as and for his last will and testament, in the presence of us, both present at the same time, who, at his request, in his presence and in the presence of each other, have hereunto subscribed our names as witnesses.

Thomas Terrific

(Testator signs here)

Ima Witness	UMA WITNESS
Witness	Witness
114 Wheat Way, Edmonton	118 Great Way, Edmonton
Address	Address
Teacher	Clerk
Occupation	Occupation

SAMPLE #4
WILL OF A SINGLE PERSON IN FAVOR
OF PARENTS FOR LIFE AND THEN EQUALLY TO
BROTHERS AND SISTERS ABSOLUTELY

THIS IS THE LAST WILL AND TESTAMENT of me, Sam Single, of the City of Lethbridge, in the Province of Alberta.

1. I REVOKE all former wills and codicils.

2. I APPOINT Paul Parent of the City of Lethbridge, in the Province of Alberta, to be the personal representative and trustee of this my will. In the event the above-named individual predeceases me or be unwilling or unable to act as my personal representative and trustee, then I HEREBY APPOINT Paula Parent to be the personal representative and trustee (hereinafter referred to as my personal representative) of this my will.

3. I GIVE all my real and personal property whatsoever and wheresoever situate including any property over which I may have a general power of appointment to my said personal representative upon the following trusts, namely:

(a) To use his discretion in the realization of my estate, with power to my personal representative to sell, call in, and convert into money any part of my estate not consisting of money at such time or times, in such manner and upon such terms, and either for cash or credit or for part cash and part credit as he may in his uncontrolled discretion decide upon, or to postpone such conversion of my estate or any part or parts thereof for such length of time as he may think best and I hereby declare that my personal representative may retain any portion of my estate in the form in which it may be at my death (notwithstanding that it may not be in the form of an investment in which trustees are authorized to invest trust funds and whether or not there is a liability attached to any such portion of my estate) for such length of time as he may in his discretion deem advisable, shall not be held responsible for any loss that may happen to my estate by reason of so doing;

(b) To pay out of the capital of my estate my just debts, funeral and testamentary expenses, and all outstanding taxes;

(c) To hold the residue of my estate in trust for my mother and father alive at my death in equal shares provided that the share of each parent of mine who shall be living at my death shall be held and kept invested by my personal representative and the income and capital or so much thereof as my personal representative in his discretion considers advisable shall be paid to or applied for the benefit of my mother and father and survivor of them.

4. UPON TRUST after the death of the survivor of my father and mother to pay the remaining residue of my estate to my brothers and sisters then living in equal shares per stirpes.

IN WITNESS WHEREOF I have hereunto set my hand this 6th day of June, 200-.

SIGNED, PUBLISHED, AND DECLARED by the said Testator, Sam Single, as and for his last will and testament, in the presence of us, both present at the same time, who, at his request, in his presence and in the presence of each other, have hereunto subscribed our names as witnesses.

Sam Single
(Testator signs here)

Ira Witness	UMA WITNESS
Witness	Witness
21 Sugar Beet Road, Lethbridge	21 Sugar Beet Road, Lethbridge
Address	Address
Farmer	Machinist
Occupation	Occupation

survivor receives only the interest on the $100 000, and not the sum of money itself. Once the survivor dies he or she has no further interest in the money. (The survivor cannot pass it under a will, for example.) The money passes to the ultimate beneficiary named in the first deceased's will.

The purpose of these provisions is to prevent assets from being squandered or to provide a means of support for someone who is not capable of managing the asset.

The following is an example of a clause that creates a life interest.

> Provided that my wife, Harriet Homee, survives me for 30 days, I direct my personal representative to permit her to use and occupy the marital home located at 222 High Street, Calgary, for the balance of her lifetime or as long as she does not remarry. Upon the death of my said wife or in the event of her remarriage, I direct my personal representative to deliver my said home to my son, Henry Homee, for his own use absolutely.

Exercise caution in creating life interests in a home-drawn will as there are problems with making such gifts enforceable and ensuring the greatest amount of tax relief for the beneficiaries.

2. Gifts to infants

No one can pay out a gift to a beneficiary who is under 18. If a gift is made to an underage beneficiary, the personal representative must hold the gift until the beneficiary reaches 18.

Alternatively, the money is paid to the Office of the Public Trustee, where it will be administered and accounted for until the infant reaches 18. Your personal representative's duty is to protect the gift for the beneficiary and to invest it to produce a reasonable but safe income during the period in which the money is held. Frequently, the personal representative is permitted to "encroach" upon the capital of an infant's gift if, in his or her discretion, the capital is needed to maintain the child.

This means that the personal representative has the power to pay out certain amounts of the gift to the infant, or to use certain amounts for the infant's benefit. As the word "benefit" has been interpreted very widely by the courts, a clause permitting a personal representative, for example, to encroach upon a gift of money for the infant's benefit permits the personal representative to pay the money out for any worthwhile cause.

Sample #5 shows a will with a trust arrangement for infant children.

3. Investments

The law of Alberta limits the kinds of investments a personal representative can make with the assets of an estate. So, if there are life interests created in a will, or if infants are beneficiaries of an estate, the personal representative must hold the gift and invest the funds until the life interest expires, or the infant reaches 18. The gift must be invested; it cannot be hidden in a mattress and then paid out when the time comes.

The personal representative is required to make only those investments that are quite safe, with the result that the return for the investment may be very low. If you wish to give your personal representative more freedom, you may do so by inserting a specific clause in the will allowing the personal representative to invest at his or her own discretion. You might use a clause like the following:

> Notwithstanding the provisions of the Trustee Act and any other law pertaining to the form of investments in which trustees are authorized to invest trust funds, I authorize my personal representative to invest any portion of my estate in such investments as he may see fit.

THIS IS THE LAST WILL AND TESTAMENT of me, Sally Lund, of the City of Red Deer, in the Province of Alberta.

1. I REVOKE all former wills and codicils.

2. I APPOINT Larry Lund of the City of Red Deer, in the Province of Alberta, to be the personal representative and trustee of this my will. Should the above-named individual predecease me or be unwilling or unable to act as my personal representative or trustee, then I HEREBY APPOINT Perry Price of the City of Red Deer, in the Province of Alberta, to be the personal representative and trustee (hereinafter referred to as my personal representative) of this my will.

3. I APPOINT Larry Lund of the City of Red Deer, in the Province of Alberta, to be the guardian of the persons and estates of my infant children during their minority. In the event that he shall predecease me or be unwilling or unable to act, then I hereby appoint Perry Price to be the guardian of the persons and estates of my infant children during their minority.

4. I GIVE all my real and personal property whatsoever and wheresoever situate including any property over which I may have a general power of appointment to my said personal representative upon the following trusts, namely:

(a) To use his discretion in the realization of my estate, with power to sell, call in, and convert into money any part of my estate not consisting of money at such time or times, in such manner and upon such terms, and either for cash or credit or for part cash and part credit as he may in his uncontrolled discretion decide upon, or to postpone such conversion of my estate or any part or parts thereof for such length of time as he may think best and I hereby declare that my personal representative may retain any portion of my estate in the form in which it may be at my death (notwithstanding that it may not be in the form of an investment in which trustees are authorized to invest trust funds and whether or not there is a liability attached to any such portion of my estate) for such length of time as he may in his discretion deem advisable, and he shall not be held responsible for any loss that may happen to my estate by reason of so doing;

(b) To pay out of the capital of my estate my just debts, funeral and testamentary expenses and all outstanding taxes;

(c) To hold the residue of my estate in trust for my issue alive at my death in equal shares per stirpes provided that the share of each child of mine who shall be living at my death shall be held and kept invested by my personal representative and the income and capital or so much thereof as my personal representative in his discretion considers advisable shall be paid to or applied for the benefit of such child until he or she attains the age of majority. When the capital of such share of the amount thereof remaining shall be paid or transferred to him or her, any income not so paid or applied in any year to be added to the capital and dealt with as part thereof, and provided further that if such child shall die before attaining the age of majority such share, or the amount thereof remaining, shall be held by my personal representative in trust for the children of such child who survive him or her in equal shares;

(d) Any payments to be made to any infant beneficiary shall be deemed sufficiently made if paid to their guardian.

IN WITNESS WHEREOF I have hereunto set my hand this 5th day of June, 200-.

SIGNED, PUBLISHED, AND DECLARED by the said Testatrix, Sally Lund, as and for her last will and testament, in the presence of us, both present at the same time, who, at her request, in her presence and in the presence of each other, have hereunto subscribed our names as witnesses.

Sally Lund
(Testatrix signs here)

Ima Witness
Witness

UMA WITNESS
Witness

110 Reader Lane,
Red Deer
Address

200 Self-Counsel Way,
Red Deer
Address

Lawyer
Occupation

Doctor
Occupation

4. Co-personal representatives

In larger estates, two or three people are often appointed co-personal representatives of the estate. The rule regarding multiple personal representatives is that all actions must be unanimously approved. If you do not wish this rule to apply to your personal representatives, and prefer that the majority rule govern, use a clause like the following:

> I hereby direct that the decision of a majority of my personal representatives shall be decisive upon any matter and the decision of the majority shall be binding on all personal representatives and beneficiaries.

In the case of the appointment of more than one personal representative to act at the same time, you may provide in your will that in the event of the death of one of them, the surviving personal representative shall appoint a replacement for the deceased personal representative.

5. A guardian

The Domestic Relations Act of Alberta specifically gives parents the right to appoint guardians. The clause in your will should take the form of a definite appointment of someone to act as guardian.

This appointment may be made in a will or in any other document as long as the words used are sufficiently clear to show a definite appointment. An oral appointment is insufficient. A deed used to appoint a guardian need not be formally executed as is required for a will.

Mere appointment cannot force anyone to act as guardian. Therefore, the guardian's approval should be obtained before the appointment. Careful consideration should be given to the following matters when choosing your guardian:

(a) The age of the children compared to the age of the guardian

(b) Lifestyle of both the parents and the guardian (The swinging single brother may not make the ideal guardian. Someone with a large family may not be able to handle more children.)

(c) The economic situation of the guardian and the estate

(d) Present religious beliefs

(e) Educational expectations for your children

(f) Any cultural considerations (e.g., language)

(g) Disciplinary attitudes to child-rearing

A typical clause used to appoint a guardian may be as follows:

> I hereby constitute and appoint my friend, Peter Piper, to be the guardian of the person and estate of my son, Gordon Growe, during his minority.

Parents should also give some thought to the necessity of putting special clauses in their wills providing for such things as the following:

(a) Immediate expenses of moving children into a new home

(b) The possible need for the guardian to buy a new home or build onto a present home in order to provide adequate living space

(c) Special health or educational requirements that dictate immediate outlays of money

(d) The right to spend income and/or encroach on capital to provide for needs of children

(e) Any wish to compensate the guardian for assuming this responsibility

Under Alberta law, the appointment of a guardian is not binding on the court. If a child is left without parents, the courts decide who shall be the guardian. A deceased parent's appointment can be completely disregarded and another person appointed as guardian. The appointment of a testamentary guardian is really no more than the fulfillment of a parental duty and a written request that named persons be the guardians for your infant children. Anyone can oppose your testamentary appointment. The court has the ultimate decision-making power in any problem revolving around guardianship. The court, when making any decisions relating to guardianship, applies the golden rule of "What is in the best interests of the child?"

6. Funeral instructions

Today, more and more people are concerned about the manner in which they are to be buried and the cost of burial. They may make wills that contain clauses directing that they be cremated or that they be buried in a certain location or through the services of a certain funeral home. Personal representatives are commonly directed to keep funeral expenses to a minimum. A simple statement to this effect is sufficient to inform the personal representative of this duty.

It is the personal representative who is responsible for looking after the body of the deceased, not the surviving spouse. If the deceased's funeral instructions in the will are not reasonable in relation to the size of the estate, then the personal representative may apply to the court to be relieved of the duty of following the instructions contained in the will.

If there are no directions whatever concerning the burial of the deceased, then the personal representative is entitled to spend a reasonable amount only for the burial. The beneficiaries may sue a personal representative for any "excess expenses" arising from extravagance or disregard for the instructions contained in the will.

7. Body donation

People commonly direct that their bodies are to be delivered to a local university or medical school for research purposes. Once the body has served its purpose, the medical school arranges for the disposition of the body at no cost to the estate of the deceased. It is necessary for everyone who wishes to donate his or her body to research to contact the particular school involved and complete a "donor card."

8. Organ transplants

Occasionally a person will wish to make certain organs of his or her body available for transplant purposes. A clause such as the following might be inserted in the will:

> It is my desire, and I so instruct my personal representative, to make any of my physical organs available for the purpose of transplant or research, provided that I expressly forbid the use of my body, as a whole, for purposes of medical research.

As well, to facilitate the donation of body parts, you should complete the appropriate section of your Alberta Health Card. Be sure to discuss these wishes with your personal representative and your family.

9. Eye bank

It is now fairly common for people to bequeath their eyes to the Eye Bank run by the Canadian National Institute for the Blind. Such a gift should be worded in the following fashion:

> Should my eyes be considered useful by the Eye Bank of Canada, I direct my personal representative to carry out the arrangements that I have made so that my eyes will be left to the Eye Bank of Canada under the auspices of the CNIB.

Arrangements for gifts like this must be made during the lifetime of the donor. Donor cards may be obtained from the Canadian National Institute for the Blind. They should be completed and a portion returned to the Institute. You carry with you your portion of the donor card as it serves to notify anyone that, in the event of your death, your eyes have been bequeathed to the Eye Bank of Canada and that immediate steps should be taken to ensure that your wishes are carried out.

In any case where the will contains directions for burial, or for the disposition of the body to medical science, or bequeaths organs or eyes, the personal representative named in the will must be advised of these provisions immediately after the will is signed. If these provisions come as a surprise after the death, it may be too late to put them into effect, since the will is often not consulted until two or three days later. Common sense should be exercised in such circumstances and steps taken to ensure that wishes of this nature are carried out.

10. Charity

You may wish to leave money to your favorite charity. Such a gift should be explicitly set out in the will. A charity is defined as any institution that is established for charitable purposes including —

(a) relief of poverty,

(b) advancement of education,

(c) advancement of religion, and

(d) other purposes beneficial to the community.

This could be worded as follows:

> I BEQUEATH THE sum of $10 000 to the governing body of Hardrock High School at Calgary for the purpose of acquiring equipment and facilities for the playing of all sports.

Be sure to identify the charity correctly. You may wish to contact them and find out the proper legal name.

11. RRSPs

Special consideration should be given to the drafting of clauses to properly handle the passing of Registered Retirement Savings Plans (RRSPs). The rules governing the tax consequences upon the death of the owner of an RRSP change with almost every federal budget, so professional advice is recommended. Some of the current rules are as follows:

(a) If a taxpayer dies before his or her RRSP matures and the beneficiary is anyone except a spouse, the value is included in the income of the deceased for the year of death. This could result in a considerably higher tax rate.

(b) If the beneficiary is a spouse, that spouse has the option of cashing the plan or rolling it over into his or her own plan, thus delaying tax payment.

(c) If death occurs after the maturity of the RRSP, the amount included in the income of the deceased for the year of death is —

> (i) the total value of the balance of the guaranteed portion of an annuity purchased with RRSP funds, plus

> (ii) the value of the property in a Registered Retirement Income Fund at death

12. Accounts receivable

If your estate is likely to include many accounts receivable, considerable tax savings can be obtained by leaving such accounts to a designated beneficiary. If the will does not specifically provide for a bequest of accounts receivable, they will be included in the income for the year of death at their face value less a reserve for bad debts.

If, however, a specific bequest is made of the receivables, then they are non-taxable in the hands of the beneficiary until the time when the beneficiary either disposes of them at a discount price or collects the receivables over a period of time. You might use the following form of clause to accomplish this:

> I DIRECT THAT my personal representative shall pay and transfer to my wife for her own use absolutely all of my accounts receivable if she survives me for a period of 30 days, provided that, if she predeceases me or survives me but dies within the period of 30 days after my death, I hereby designate my son as recipient.

13. Use of a memorandum

If you have a long list of specific bequests to make, you can list these in a memorandum. In order for the memorandum to be binding, it must be referred to in your will and signed by you. The memorandum then becomes part of the will and is subject to the same rules. It can only be amended by means of a codicil or a new will.

f. WHAT ABOUT DEBTS?

A will usually provides that the personal representative shall pay all the debts of the deceased outstanding at the time of death. Such a provision is not essential since it is the legal obligation of all personal representatives to pay the debts of the estate before distributing anything to beneficiaries. Hence, no specific direction in the will is needed to carry this out. In addition, a personal representative is obliged to pay all fees in connection with probating the will, all funeral expenses, and all legal fees before paying out bequests under the will. If there are insufficient assets of the estate to pay all these items, the law provides for priorities of payment.

There may be sufficient assets of the estate to cover all the debts and expenses outlined above, but the assets may be insufficient to pay all the specific bequests and gifts of money. In this event, the assets that remain after payment of debts will be divided among the beneficiaries proportionately according to the amounts they would have received had the assets been

sufficient. Of course, in this situation the residuary beneficiary would not receive anything because there would be no
residue.

g. CAN YOU DISINHERIT A DEPENDANT?

As a general rule, people have the utmost freedom in disposing of their assets under a will. You may choose not to leave
anything to your relatives and leave everything to charity; or
you may leave it all to one child, cutting out another. In other
words, you have complete testamentary freedom, subject to
the exceptions imposed by the Family Relief Act and the
Matrimonial Property Act. These acts allow the courts to
interfere with the provisions of the will of a deceased person
in certain narrow circumstances.

If an application is made to the courts by a "dependant"
and if that dependant can show that the will of the deceased
has not made "adequate provision" for that dependant, the
court will interfere with the provisions of the will and order
something to be paid out of the estate to the dependant.

A dependant can also apply to the court where there is no
will and his or her share under the Intestate Succession Act is
inadequate.

A "dependant" is the husband or wife of the deceased
person, or a child under 18 years of age, or a child over 18 years
of age who because of mental or physical handicap is unable to
earn a livelihood. A husband or wife of the deceased may
include a former spouse because of the Matrimonial Property
Act of Alberta. Special consideration must be given to former
spouses if a matrimonial property settlement has not been
drawn in such a way that a former spouse has waived his or her
rights under the above act. Only people from this group of
individuals can apply through the courts to interfere with the
provisions of the will and the distribution of the estate.

An action under the Matrimonial Property Act can be
made or continued by a surviving spouse after the death of

the other spouse only if an application could have been commenced immediately before the death. Thus, if a husband and wife were living together in relative harmony and upon the husband's death the wife discovers that she has been left only a small portion of the husband's estate, her remedy lies with the Family Relief Act, not the Matrimonial Property Act. She would not have been able to bring an application under the Matrimonial Property Act immediately *before* her husband's death because they were not separated, so she therefore cannot bring an application under that act *after* the death.

"Adequate provision" is a rather uncertain term and I will not attempt to define it here. The effect of the Family Relief Act may be summed up by saying, for example, that should a man attempt to exclude his wife completely from his will when he has always supported her and she has no substantial assets of her own, an application by the wife would likely be successful. The court would award her either a lump-sum payment or a periodic payment for the balance of her life.

It should be emphasized that in the case of a successful application under the Family Relief Act, the will is not declared invalid. It remains perfectly valid. The effect of a court order is to interfere with the provisions of the will to provide for a suitable payment to the dependant. The result is that one or more beneficiaries under the will receives less than he or she would have if no application had been made by the dependant.

Exercise caution if you intend to attempt to disinherit a spouse or child. (The usual practice is to list the reasons for disinheritance in the will and these reasons must not be frivolous.) In any case, legal advice is necessary because of the complexities involved in interpreting the Family Relief Act and the various court decisions that have been decided under it. Certainly no attempt should be made in a home-drawn will to avoid the act without some legal assistance. It should be emphasized that in many circumstances it will be simply impossible to disinherit the spouse or child. A "spouse" may also have rights under the Matrimonial Property Act. Also, the Dower Act gives to a surviving spouse the right to live in the matrimonial home for the rest of his or her life.

h. HOW TO MAKE CHANGES IN A WILL

The situation often arises where a person has made a will some years earlier and circumstances change so that he or she now wishes to make minor alterations in it. Instead of making a completely new will, it is possible to simply make a "codicil." A codicil is an amendment to the will, stating that certain provisions of the will are now to be revoked. A codicil may also substitute new provisions for the revoked provisions (see Sample #6).

A codicil is commonly used when a beneficiary or the person named as personal representative dies during the lifetime of the person making the will. The will should be revised to reflect the changed circumstances.

A codicil, like a will, is a testamentary document and all the rules outlined earlier in this chapter about making a will apply to a codicil. When you make a codicil you must have two witnesses to your signature. These witnesses need not be the original witnesses to the will.

A codicil should start with the words:

> This is a codicil to the last will of me, Jon J.
> John, of the City of Calgary in the Province of
> Alberta, which said last will bears date the 7th
> day of January 200-.

It is important to tie together the original will and the codicil which amends it by referring to the date of the will in the opening words of the codicil. The codicil should then go on to state which clauses are revoked or amended and if a new provision is being substituted for one that has been revoked. The codicil should always state that you confirm the will in all other respects.

THIS IS THE FIRST CODICIL to the last will of me, Sarah Surprise, which last will bears the date of the 13th day of May, 200-.

1. I DIRECT that the first paragraph of Clause Three be deleted and the following clause be substituted therefore:

In the event my said husband, Sol Surprise, shall predecease me or surviving me shall die within a period of 30 days following my decease, I APPOINT my daughter, Sue Surprise, to be the personal representative of this my will.

2. I REVOKE Clause Five (a) of my said last will.

3. I DIRECT that the following clause be added to my said will.

I give, devise, and bequeath to my daughter, Sue Surprise, the following items of jewellery and china.

- a) My Australian opal pendant
- b) My jade earrings and pin set
- c) My diamond necklace
- d) My Moorcroft vase
- e) My Royal Doulton tea set
- f) My Royal Doulton figurine collection

4. In all other respects, I confirm my said last will.

IN WITNESS WHEREOF, I, Sarah Surprise, have to this first codicil to my last will contained on this single sheet of paper subscribed my name at the City of Edmonton, in the Province of Alberta, on this 20th day of June, 200-.

SIGNED, PUBLISHED, AND DECLARED by the said Sarah Surprise, the above-named Testatrix, as and for this first codicil to her last will, in the presence of us, who, in her presence, at her request, and in the presence of each other have hereunto sub-scribed our names as wit-nesses, attesting the same.

Sarah Surprise
_____
(Testatrix signs here)

Ima Witness
_____
Witness

603 North Avenue,
Edmonton
_____
Address

Nurse
_____
Occupation

UMA WITNESS
_____
Witness

306 South Avenue,
Edmonton
_____
Address

Engineer
_____
Occupation

The effect of making a codicil is that the will and the codicil are read together and any amendments contained in the codicil are read into the will as though they had appeared there in the first place. A series of codicils may be made and in each instance the changes in each codicil will be read into the original will. If too many changes are made, a new will should be prepared incorporating all of the changes to date. This helps avoid possible confusion with dates.

i. HOW OFTEN SHOULD A WILL BE REVISED?

Once a will has been made, it should be reviewed at least every five years, and more frequently if there is a death among the beneficiaries.

There is no law requiring that a will be revised from time to time. A will 50 years old is perfectly valid and will be effective to pass on the assets of the estate. The reason for reviewing and revising your will is a practical one rather than a legal one. Over the years, friendships change, relations die, and the value of your estate may change considerably. In larger estates, changes in tax laws may prompt a change in the will in order to minimize income taxes. Remember, a marriage automatically revokes any will made prior to the marriage unless the will was made in contemplation of the marriage. A divorce, however, does not automatically revoke a will.

For all these reasons, you should review your will regularly and, if it no longer makes appropriate provisions for the existing situation, revise it.

Remember, minor amendments can be made by way of a simple codicil. If the changes are major, a new will should be drawn up. The new will should expressly revoke the earlier will. Many lawyers recommend that when a new will is signed, the former will be physically destroyed. This may have its disadvantages if, for some reason, the later will proves invalid. In such circumstances, the former will might be reviewed and ruled valid by a court. It may, therefore, be advisable to retain both the old and new wills together.

j. HOW TO REVOKE A WILL

If a person destroys the original will or tears it up fully intending to revoke it, then the effect of the destruction or tearing up is to revoke the will. Should the person then die without having made a new will, the estate will be distributed as though the will that was destroyed had never existed.

As previously mentioned, a will is revoked by the making of a new will that is either inconsistent with the former will or that expressly revokes the former will. The most recent will always governs.

Should you wish to revoke an existing will, but it is impractical or impossible for you to destroy it, since the will is, for example, in your safety deposit box at the bank, you may make a codicil to that effect. The codicil states that your last will and testament is revoked in all respects, and you identify the will being revoked by referring to the date on which it was signed (see Sample #7).

This codicil must be signed like any other codicil, that is, in the presence of two witnesses. Once signed, it effectively revokes the earlier will.

k. MARRIAGE AND WILLS

Every will is automatically revoked by marriage except in certain narrow circumstances. Upon marrying, you should make a new will as soon as possible.

A will is not revoked by marriage when the will was made prior to marriage and in contemplation of the specific marriage. The will should state on its face that it is being prepared in contemplation of your marriage to a certain named person. If it does so, the will will not be revoked by subsequent marriage to that person. Sample #8 shows the opening of a will made in contemplation of marriage.

SAMPLE #7
CODICIL REVOKING WILL

This is the second codicil to the last will of me, Tony Testator, whose last will bears the date of the 25th day of July, 1987.

1. I revoke in all respects my last will and testament which bears the date of the 25th of July, 1987.

2. I further revoke in all respects the first codicil to my said will, which codicil bears the date of the 16th day of September, 1995.

In witness whereof I, Tony Testator, have to this second codicil to my last will contained on this single sheet of paper subscribed my name at the City of Calgary in the Province of Alberta, on this 30th day of April, 200-.

SIGNED, PUBLISHED, AND DECLARED by the said Tony Testator the above named Testator as and for the second codicil to his last will and testament, in the presence of us, who in his presence, at his request and in the presence of each other, have hereunto subscribed our names as witnesses attesting. ~

Tony Testator
_____
(Testator signs here)

Ima Witnen
_____
Witness

I. C. Eve
_____
Witness

107 Probate Row,
_____
Address

105 Probate Row,
_____
Address

Clerk
_____
Occupation

Saleswoman
_____
Occupation

SAMPLE #8
WILL MADE IN CONTEMPLATION
OF MARRIAGE

THIS IS THE LAST WILL AND TESTAMENT of me, Tom Terror, of the City of Calgary, in the Province of Alberta, made in contemplation of my marriage to Terri Toomuch.

1. I HEREBY REVOKE all wills and codicils.

2. IF MY MARRIAGE to the said Terri Toomuch shall be solemnized, I nominate, constitute, and appoint the said Terri Toomuch sole personal representative and trustee of this my will. But if she should predecease me or die within a period of 30 days following my decease, then on the death of the survivor of me and the said Terri Toomuch, or, if my marriage to the said Terri Toomuch shall not be solemnized, I appoint Nathan Noone (hereinafter referred to as my personal representative) to be the personal representative and trustee of this my will in the place of the said Terri Toomuch.*

---

*Note: This will then proceeds to give the trustees instructions as to distribution as in other examples.

1. WHAT HAPPENS IF YOU MOVE TO ANOTHER PROVINCE?

All the English-speaking provinces have wills legislation similar to Alberta with minor exceptions. For example, Manitoba and Saskatchewan recognize holograph wills (entirely handwritten without witnesses) while British Columbia does not. Quebec, however, operates under different laws altogether, so if you are moving to or from there, you will need to make a new will.

Also, if you have assets in "foreign" jurisdictions, upon your death your estate will have to pass through probate in all the jurisdictions in which those assets are located (technically this is called "resealing of letters probate") unless you form a small holding company in your province of residence to hold all the assets. In this case, you can merely pass on the shares of the company to your beneficiaries, and thereby avoid all the trouble and expense of the resealing problem. Legal advice is strongly recommended in this case.

A third reason for preparing a new will after moving is that, upon your death, there is considerable detailed work to be done by your personal representative and, if he or she is residing out of the province, the task is even more difficult. Further, if children are involved, a bond may have to be posted. So, for simplicity, it is better for you to appoint at least one locally resident personal representative, which involves changing your will, or at least executing a codicil.

m. PERSONAL DIRECTIVES ACT

The Personal Directives Act came into effect in Alberta in 1997. This act allows Albertans to give legally binding personal directions by writing instructions and/or naming agents to make personal decisions on their behalf if they become incapacitated. Prior to the passing of the Personal Directive Act, Albertans did not have the legal means to provide instructions for future personal decisions related to their care. The act was designed to give individuals the opportunity to extend their right to self-determination over personal matters in the event of future incapacity. It allows an individual to choose now for the future. A personal directive is needed most by those who have been diagnosed with an illness that will affect their decision-making ability. However, anyone can suffer a sudden loss of ability so the personal directive is a forward planning tool relevant to all individuals.

A personal directive will provide for all personal matters relating to care, living conditions, and medical treatment but not financial matters. Financial matters require an enduring power of attorney under the Power of Attorney Act. Therefore, to be fully prepared for your care and eventual death you should have a personal directive (for personal care), an enduring power of attorney (for financial matters) and a will (to dispose of your assets upon death). The Alberta government has provided us with all the tools, now it remains with us to use them. If these tools are used, fewer and fewer applications will be necessary under the Dependent Adult's Act.

1. What is a personal directive?

It is a written document which gives instructions and/or names an agent and gives the agent authority to make decisions in the event you become incapacitated. There is no special form to use.

The requirements for a valid personal directive are quite simple. It must be —

(a) in writing,

(b) dated,

(c) signed at the end in the presence of a witness or, if someone signs on behalf of the maker, signed in the presence of the maker, and

(d) signed by the witness in the presence of the maker.

A personal directive may contain information and instructions respecting any personal matters, including the following:

(a) Designation of agents and their authority

(b) Designating one or more persons to determine the maker's capacity

(c) Naming the persons who are and the persons who are not to be notified of the coming into effect of the personal directive

(d) Providing instructions with respect to access to confidential information about the maker

The personal directive cannot be used to give instructions about assisted suicide or euthanasia.

If you make a personal directive, you should advise your doctor, lawyer, and religious advisor. You may also want to carry a card saying you have a personal directive and who should be called in case of an emergency. For better tracking one should only execute one original personal directive and then number the copies keeping a record of where the copies are. Persons who should have copies include agents named in the directive, health care providers, your lawyer, and members of your family.

2. Who is an agent?

An agent is the person designated in a personal directive to make personal decisions on behalf of the maker. This is often a spouse, a child, or a trusted friend. The agent must be at least 18 years old, and willing and capable of making the required decisions. More than one agent can be appointed. The responsibilities of the agent cease if —

(a) the maker regains capacity,

(b) the maker specified a date or circumstance when the personal directive would be revoked or changed,

(c) the maker dies,

(d) the court determines the personal directive has expired, or

(e) the agent no longer wishes to act.

3. When does a personal directive come into effect?

The appointment of the agent in the personal directive comes into effect when the maker becomes incapacitated. The Personal Directive Act defines capacity as "the ability to understand the information that is relevant to the making of a personal decision and the ability to appreciate the reasonably foreseeable consequences of the decision." Incapacity does not mean that a person has a mental disorder. It merely means that a person is unable to understand the nature or effect of his or her decisions after receiving adequate explanation of the options.

To implement a personal directive, the maker must be assessed as lacking capacity. The determination of capacity can be done by —

(a) the person named in the personal directive after consulting with a physician or psychologist, or

(b) two service providers, at least one of whom must be a physician or psychologist, who must make a written declaration that the maker lacks capacity.

The declaration of incapacity must be kept by the physician or psychologist and a copy must be given to the maker, the maker's agent, and any other person designated in the maker's personal directive. The agent must, subject to specific directions in the personal directive, make every reasonable effort to notify the nearest relatives and the legal representative of the maker that the personal directive is in effect. For example, an attorney under an enduring power of attorney must be contacted.

4. What form should a personal directive take?

Sample #9 sets out a very simple personal directive. It can be expanded to fit an individual's needs. Some of the things that should be considered are:

(a) *Agent.* It may be preferable to name your spouse as the primary agent. You may name someone to act alone or jointly with another person.

(b) *Alternative Agent.* In case the person you name as your agent dies, you should name an alternate.

(c) *Decisions.* Specify the types of decisions you want your agent to make. For example, your agent could make decisions for you regarding:

PERSONAL DIRECTIVE OF POLLY SMITH

This Personal Directive is given by me, POLLY SMITH, of the City of Grande Prairie, in the Province of Alberta on _____ day of _____, 20____.

1.   I revoke any Personal Directives or living wills or equivalent documents that I have already made

2.

2.1 I appoint my spouse, JAMES SMITH, of 111 — First Street, Grande Prairie, Alberta to act as my Agent pursuant to the Personal Directives Act (Alberta).

2.2 If my spouse refuses or is unable to act as my health care agent, then I appoint my daughter, SUSIE SMITH, of Sundry, Alberta to be my Agent.

3.

3.1 This Directive shall come into affect only when I lack capacity to make a decision about personal matters.

3.2 I will lack capacity when:

(a)   my Agent signs a written declaration to that effect after consulting with a physician or psychologist; or

(b)   if my Agent is unwilling or unable to sign such a declaration then when two service providers, at least one of whom is a physician or psychologist, sign a written declaration to that effect.

4.

4.1 My Agent has authority to make personal decisions on my behalf.

4.2 In this Personal Directive, personal decisions include any matters of a non-financial nature that relate to my person and without limitation includes decisions as to:

(a)   health care;

(b)   accommodations;

(c)   with whom I may live and associate;

(d) my participation in social, educational, and employment activities; and

(e) legal matters that do not relate to my estate.

5.　　　　I direct my Agent to use my resources to allow me to live independently for as long as possible in my own home or if I must be in institutional care to ensure that I receive the best possible care within my resources. If this depletes all of my resources such that I have no estate left when I die, this is acceptable.

6.　　　　My Agent must instruct my health care service providers based on the following guidelines:

(a) In the event of a catastrophic illness for which there is no cure, I would like comfort measures only, including surgery if needed, to relieve symptoms. Treat the illness for relief of distress, not to prolong life. I want to stay at home if possible, with transfer to hospital only for uncomfortable discomfort;

(b) I do not want to prolong life at all costs. I hereby give authorization for the withholding or withdrawal of treatment if my physician and my Agent determine that my death is imminent with no reasonable medical expectation of recovery, whether or not life sustaining procedures are utilized. In addition, I must have lost the ability to interact with others with no reasonable chance of regaining that ability. My physician and my Agent are instructed to determine the meaning of the term *reasonable* as used in the two previous sentences;

(c) Should I be mentally incapable, I do not want to have my life prolonged because everything meaningful in life to me will have already passed. In that situation, I refuse consent to ordinary or heroic techniques that artificially maintain a life sustaining function of my body and are used only to prolong my life without improving the chances for cure or reversal of my condition.

7.　　　　My Agent has the right to be provided with all information and records including medical records that are relevant to me, my medical care, my personal decision to be made at any given time, or the determination of capacity, without restriction.

8.   If, in the opinion of my Agent, this directive does not give clear instructions that are relevant to the health care decision to be made on my behalf, my Agent must make the decision based upon my Agent's knowledge of my wishes, beliefs and values.

I make this Personal Directive as to the date first written above.

Tom Jones

Witness

Polly Smith

POLLY SMITH

AFFIDAVIT OF EXECUTION

CANADA	)	I, TOM JONES
PROVINCE OF ALBERTA	)	of the City of Grande
TO WIT:	)	Prairie, in the Province
	)	of Alberta
	)	MAKE OATH AND SAY:

1.   I WAS PERSONALLY present and did see POLLY SMITH, named in the within instrument, who is personally known to me to be the person named therein, duly sign and execute the same for the purposes named therein.

2.   THE SAME was executed at the City of Grande Prairie, in the Province of Alberta, and that I am the subscribing witness thereto.

3.   I KNOW the said POLLY SMITH and she is, in my belief, of the full age of eighteen (18) years.

SWORN BEFORE ME at the City of   )
Grande Prairie, in the Province of Alberta,   )
this _____ day of _____, 20_____.   )

_____*Tom Jones*_____   )
TOM JONES

_____*Bill Rogers*_____
A COMMISSIONER FOR OATHS   )
in and for the Province of Alberta   )

- health care
- accommodation
- with whom you live and associate
- legal matters (other than estate)
- your style of living — social, educational, and employment activities

You should also list restrictions that you want placed on the above decisions and name any persons you may want to monitor your agent's decisions.

For more information on personal directives see *Your Personal Directive*, another book in the Self-Counsel Series.

n. PROBLEMS

A will may, of course, be made by someone who cannot write. In such a case, verbal instructions can be written down. Before the will is signed, it must be read over in full to the person making it, who may then put his or her "mark" on it. This is usually an X. One of the witnesses should then indicate beside the X that it is the mark of the testator. The witnesses then proceed to sign the will as in the normal case.

As we discussed earlier, a "holograph will" is one that is written completely in the handwriting of the person making it and signed without any witnesses to the signature. A will of this sort is recognized in Alberta as an alternative to a will with two witnesses, because it is completely in the handwriting of the person making it. But a personal representative may have problems with such a will and it should be avoided if possible. You cannot make a valid holograph will by filling in the blanks of a stationer's form.

o. SUMMARY OF STEPS IN THE EXECUTION OF A WILL

If you wish to make your own will, use the following points as a summary of various matters you should bear in mind.

(a) Jot down on a piece of paper your debts and your assets. Make a list of those you wish to benefit under your will. Prepare a brief statement showing who your beneficiaries are to be and precisely what they are to receive.

(b) You are now in a position to start drafting your will. You may either type your own or use a will form (available from the publisher; see order form at the front of the book) and adapt it according to the instructions and examples shown in this chapter. Be sure that your handwriting is clear. The will should be typed, if at all possible. If not, print.

(c) Consult the person or persons whom you propose to name as personal representative in advance, so that you can be sure that they are prepared to assume the duty in the event of your death. It is pointless to make a will naming someone as a personal representative when you know that he or she is not prepared to assume the responsibility. Take similar precautions with your proposed alternative personal representative. Remember, everyone should name an alternative personal representative if at all possible.

(d) After you have written or typed your will in which you dispose of all your assets and appoint a personal representative, sign the document. Needless to say, if you do not sign your will it will have no significance whatever at the time of your death. Two witnesses are required, and remember that they should not be beneficiaries under the will or the spouses of beneficiaries.

(e) You and the two witnesses get together in the same room. You should, in the presence of the two witnesses and with the two witnesses watching you, sign at the end of the will on the line provided there for your signature. The two witnesses should then each sign in the spaces provided for their signatures. In the event that the will is longer than one page, you and the two witnesses should initial each page of the will with the exception of the page upon which the signatures already appear. This prevents the fraudulent substitution of pages after the will has been properly signed.

(f) At the end of the will insert the date on which it is signed. This is essential, especially in cases where you have made more than one will. If one of the wills is undated, it becomes impossible to tell which will governs the disposition of your estate. No will should be signed without the day, month, and year being stated clearly.

(g) You should sign only one copy of the will. Several copies of the will might be typed or written and it is always a good idea to deliver an unsigned copy of the will to your personal representative. This allows him or her to become familiar with its provisions and, upon your death, to have immediate access to a copy of the will.

The original signed will should be kept in a safe place, like a safety deposit box.

p. ENDURING POWERS OF ATTORNEY

At common law, a power of attorney terminates on the mental incapacity of the donor. This rule is questionable as it extinguishes the attorney's power at the very time that it is needed. To alleviate this problem, the Alberta Legislature has passed the Power of Attorney Act which allows enduring powers of attorney (EPA). An EPA provides a simple means for people to provide for their own incapacity. It is a vehicle to be used to appoint an attorney whose powers will continue during the donor's incapacity. Sample #10 shows an enduring power of attorney and the other documents that must accompany it.

In order for a power of attorney to be an enduring power of attorney, it must —

(a) be in writing;

(b) be dated;

SAMPLE #10
ENDURING POWER OF ATTORNEY

ENDURING POWER OF ATTORNEY

THIS POWER OF ATTORNEY is given by me, Sue Brown, of the City of Airdrie, in the Province of Alberta, on the 6th day of August, 200- .

1.   REVOKE any previous powers of attorney granted by me.

2.   APPOINT Heather Low, of the City of Calgary, in the Province of Alberta, and in the event of death or refusal or inability of Heather Low to continue to act, I APPOINT Tom Low of the City of Calgary, in the Province of Alberta, to be my attorney in accordance with the *Powers of Attorney Act* of Alberta (herein referred to as my "Attorney").

3.   My attorney has authority to do anything on my behalf that I may lawfully do by an attorney.

4.   This Power of Attorney is not subject to any conditions or restrictions.

5.   This Power of Attorney shall continue notwithstanding that after the execution of this Power of Attorney, I may become incapable or infirm.

6.   This Power of Attorney incorporates the explanatory notes in the attached schedule.

          DATED at the City of Airdrie, in the Province of Alberta, on the date first above written.

SIGNED, SEALED,
& DELIVERED   )
in the presence of:)
)
)
  Ima Witness   )   *Sue Brown*
  Witness as to the signature   )   (Seal)
  of Sue Brown   )

AFFIDAVIT OF EXECUTION

CANADA	)	I, Ima Witness
PROVINCE OF ALBERTA	)	of the City of Airdrie
TO WIT:	)	in the Province of Alberta
	)	MAKE OATH AND SAY:

1.   I WAS PERSONALLY present and did see Sue Brown, named in the within instrument, who is personally known to me to be the person named therein, duly sign and execute the same for the purposes named therein.

2.   THAT THE SAME was executed at the City of Airdrie in the Province of Alberta, and that I am the subscribing witness thereto.

3.   THAT I KNOW the said Sue Brown and she is, in my belief, of the full age of 18 years.

SWORN BEFORE ME at the City of   )
Airdrie, in the Province of Alberta,)
this 7th day of August, 200-.   )
)
Bernie Smith   ) _Ima Witness_
A COMMISSIONER FOR OATHS   )
in and for the Province of Alberta   )
Bernie Smith. My Commission expires)
September 1, 200-.   )

(c) be signed:

   (i) by the donor in the presence of a witness, or

   (ii) if the donor is physically unable to sign, by another person on behalf of the donor, at the donor's direction and in the presence of both the donor and a witness;

(d) be signed by a witness in the presence of the donor; and

(e) contain a statement indicating that either:

   (i) it is to continue despite any mental incapacity or infirmity of the donor that occurs after the execution of the power of attorney; or

   (ii) it is to take effect only on the mental incapacity or infirmity of the donor.

It is critical that you exercise great care in choosing the individual who will be your attorney as you are placing a great deal of power and trust in that person. You must decide whether your enduring power of attorney is to take effect immediately or only when you become incapacitated. This latter form is called a "springing" enduring power of attorney.

An enduring power of attorney gives your attorney the power to deal with your property and all financial matters. Your attorney will also be able to use your property to care for your spouse and dependent children. Unless you indicate otherwise, your attorney has very broad powers. You may want to impose restrictions or guidelines on your attorney's powers.

Once the enduring power of attorney takes effect, your attorney will have a duty to manage your affairs and will not be able to resign without first obtaining permission from the court. The enduring power of attorney comes to an end if you or your attorney dies.

At last we have a straightforward method by which to choose someone we feel will have our best interests in mind if we become incapacitated. You can now have a sense of confidence that you have exercised some management of your affairs should incapacity strike. As our population ages, a properly drafted and executed enduring power of attorney will become as necessary as a valid will.

3
PROBATE

The rest of this book deals with the steps taken when a death occurs; that is, the steps involved in the administration of an estate. This does not necessarily mean that after reading the book, you will be qualified to administer an estate without legal counsel. Rather, it is hoped that you will develop an understanding of the basic procedures involved and appreciate whether or not good legal counsel is needed. In the case of small, uncomplicated estates, you may be in a position to complete properly the various returns and applications required when an individual dies.

At the end of this chapter are samples of some of the forms needed to process a hypothetical estate. This example is followed through the remainder of the book to illustrate the various steps that have to be taken, but the book cannot and does not attempt to deal with every possible problem that may arise in a particular estate situation. (A more detailed explanation of the probate procedure is contained in *Probate Guide for Alberta*, another title in the Self-Counsel Series.)

a. WHAT IS PROBATE?

Before entering a lengthy discussion of the duties of a personal representative in the administration of an estate, it is necessary to define some terms. "Probate" is the procedure by which the will of the deceased person is approved by the court as a valid and last will of the deceased. It also confirms the appointment of the person named in the will as personal representative. The procedure is not required to validate the will or to make the appointment of the personal representative: it merely confirms the validity and appointment.

b. WHAT ARE THE DUTIES OF A PERSONAL REPRESENTATIVE?

A personal representative is a person appointed in a will to obtain legal title to all the assets of the deceased and to pay all the liabilities of the estate out of those assets. Then, after probate (the confirming of the appointment), with the authorization of the will, he or she distributes the balance of the assets (after *all debts* for administration, the funeral, taxes, and fees have been paid) to the beneficiaries.

The first duty of a personal representative is to obtain the original of the will and ensure that it is kept in a safe place. The next step is to assemble certain information about the deceased and his or her assets, often found in safety deposit boxes. It will be necessary to go to the bank or other institution where the safety deposit box is and show the official a copy of the will indicating that you are the personal representative. The safety deposit box will then be opened. At this time it is necessary to make a detailed list of the contents of the box with special attention being given to recording the correct number of bonds, shares, insurance policies, etc. Only after probate is completed is a personal representative able to obtain the contents of the safety deposit box. If the original will is in the safety deposit box, it is the only thing that can be removed prior to the Grant of Probate.

From that point on, the personal representative will be working with a lawyer completing all documentation for court purposes. A detailed checklist follows.

c. CHECKLIST FOR THE PERSONAL REPRESENTATIVE

The following is a list of duties of the personal representative when administering an estate. Some of the items have already been discussed, and the rest will be dealt with later in the book. This list is by no means comprehensive. It should merely serve as a guideline if you are involved in the task of administering an estate. You may also want to consider these tasks when you are appointing a personal representative to probate your will.

Each particular estate situation will vary and new considerations will enter the picture. The number of items in this list and the complexity of many of these items will illustrate the value of competent legal assistance in the administration of an estate if it is at all complicated.

After obtaining the original will and codicil, the personal representative should order two copies of the death certificate from a local Registry Office. Each certificate costs $27.49 (cost at the time of writing). The personal representative then has the following duties, as set out in the Surrogate Court Rules:

(a) Making arrangements for the disposition of the body and for funeral, memorial, or other similar services

(b) Determining the names and addresses of those beneficially entitled to the estate property and notifying them of their interests

(c) Arranging with a bank, trust company, or other financial institution for a list of the contents of a safety deposit box

(d) Determining the full nature and value of property and debts of the deceased as at the date of death and compiling a list, including the value of all land and buildings and a summary of outstanding mortgages, leases, and other encumbrances

(e) Examining existing insurance policies, advising insurance companies of the death and placing additional insurance, if necessary

(f) Protecting or securing the safety of any estate property

(g) Providing for the protection and supervision of vacant land and buildings

(h) Arranging for the proper management of the estate property, including continuing business operations, taking control of property, and selling property

(i) Retaining a lawyer (if necessary) to advise on the administration of the estate, to apply for a grant from the court, or to bring any matter before the court

(j) Applying for any pensions, annuities, death benefits, life insurance, or other benefits payable to the estate

(k) Advising any joint tenancy beneficiaries of the death of the deceased

(l) Advising any designated beneficiaries of their interests under life insurance or other property passing outside the will

(m) Arranging for the payment of debts and expenses owed by the deceased and the estate

(n) Determining whether to advertise for claimants, checking all claims, and making payments as funds become available

(o) Taking the steps necessary to finalize the amount payable if the legitimacy or amount of a debt is in issue

(p) Determining the income tax or other tax liability of the deceased and of the estate, filing the necessary returns, paying any tax owing, and obtaining income tax or other tax clearance certificates before distributing the estate property

(q) Instructing a lawyer in any litigation

(r) Administering any continuing testamentary trusts or trusts for minors

(s) Preparing the personal representative's financial statements, a proposed compensation schedule, and a proposed final distribution schedule

(t) Distributing the estate property in accordance with the will or intestate succession provisions

At present, in Alberta there are no succession duty taxes — federal or provincial — on the value of an estate of a deceased person. However, income tax is still payable on the deceased's earnings, and capital gains tax is payable in certain circumstances by the estate or the beneficiaries. Furthermore, if the estate earns income in the period before it is distributed to beneficiaries, tax is payable on the income.

There is also a probate fee set in relation to the value of the estate that must be paid after receiving the Grant of Probate or Administration. These fees for dealing with estate applications are —

(a) Estate value of $10 000 or under — $25

(b) Over $10 000 but under $25 000 — $100

(c) Over $25 000 but under $50 000 — $200

(d) Over $50 000 but under $100 000 — $400

(e) Over $100 000 but under $250 000 — $600

(f) Over $250 000 but under $500 000 — $1 500

(g) Over $500 000 but under $1 000 000 — $3 000

(h) Over $1 000 000 — $6 000

d. WHAT HAPPENS TO JOINTLY OWNED PROPERTY?

Property of any type that is owned jointly by two or more persons (the family home is a common example) passes by what is called the right of survivorship. This means that the title to the property passes completely and irrevocably on death to the surviving joint tenant(s). This type of property passes automatically on death and it does not matter what the will says or even if there is one in existence. This asset will not be disposed of under the will.

Theoretically then, a person could place all of his or her property into joint names (including bank accounts) and not have to worry about a will. However, for a number of practical reasons this is not often done. First, most people want to leave property to more than one person. Second, the problem of drawing up joint ownership documents for personal items would be inconvenient to say the least. Third, most people are constantly acquiring new items of worth and they would be forced to revise the list every few months. As a result, it is much easier and more effective to draw up a good will.

Note: A bank account in joint names with right of survivorship enables the survivor to withdraw the balance in the account without having to go through any paperwork.

e. WHICH JUDICIAL DISTRICT DO YOU APPLY IN?

The rules of court provide that an Application for Probate shall be filed —

(a) in the judicial district where the deceased resided on the date of death, unless the court permits otherwise, or

(b) if the deceased resided outside Alberta, immediately before dying, in any judicial district where the deceased had property on the date of death.

The judicial districts of Alberta are Peace River, Edmonton, Grand Prairie, Vegreville, Wetaskiwin, Red Deer, Calgary, Drumheller, Hanna, Medicine Hat, Lethbridge, and MacLeod. If you are unsure of which judicial district the deceased resided in, or held land in, go to your nearest court house and ask.

f. WHAT ABOUT A BOND?

Generally, as the law is concerned that the personal representative carry out his or her duties properly, it is necessary to post a bond as security where the executor is not a resident of Alberta. These bonds are issued by bonding companies which charge a premium, much like an insurance policy. The cost of the bond is paid out of the proceeds of the estate.

The rule is waived if the personal representative is an Alberta resident or if there are two or more personal representatives and at least one of them is resident in Alberta. Therefore, it is simpler for probating if you appoint at least one Alberta resident as personal representative for your estate.

If a bond is required, it must be from an insurer licensed under the Insurance Act to undertake guarantee insurance as defined in that act. A bond must be for an amount equal to the gross value of the deceased's property in Alberta less, if the court orders, any amount distributable to the personal representative as beneficiary.

Rule 29 of the Surrogate Rules permits an application to be made to dispense with the filing of a bond or to reduce the amount of the bond. The main concern of the court in considering one of these applications will be the amount of assets and liabilities of the estate.

g. LACK OF SUFFICIENT FUNDS IN THE ESTATE

If there are not sufficient assets to cover all the gifts to beneficiaries, the legacies are reduced proportionately with the residuary beneficiary receiving nothing.

In cases where the assets do not even cover the immediate debts, the priority of payment is as follows:

(a) Funeral expenses

(b) Probate or administration fees

(c) Taxes due the federal government

    (d) Debts due third parties at the time of death and these in turn will be ranked as secured or unsecured

    (e) Personal representative's fees

h. THE TIME PERIOD FOR DISTRIBUTION

The ordinary rule is that after the granting of Letters Probate or the appointment of the administrator (see chapter 4 on administration), the gifts have to be distributed within one year.

If the specific gifts are not distributed within the one-year period, interest at the rate of 5% per year will accumulate on them. This interest will be deducted from the amounts paid the residuary beneficiaries so these beneficiaries would be wise to check periodically on the executor or administrator to make sure the paperwork is proceeding according to schedule.

Everyone probating or administering an estate should keep accurate records of all disbursements and assets so that the beneficiaries may receive an accounting if they want it.

A separate estate bank account should be established so that all disbursements can be paid by cheque from this account, which serves to keep an accurate record. (A disbursement is a fee that a personal representative or administrator must pay when filing or registering documents for example.)

Copies of the statement of account should be sent to all the beneficiaries along with a form that releases the personal representative from liability for paying the fees and a letter explaining that any beneficiary who does not agree with the accounts may make an application to the Surrogate Court to have the accounts reviewed. If all the beneficiaries concur with the accounts and return the releases, the legacies may be distributed.

i. FEES OF PERSONAL REPRESENTATIVES

Generally, all personal representatives are entitled to a fee from the assets of the estate and to be reimbursed for money spent in carrying out their duties.

Personal representatives may receive fair and reasonable compensation for their responsibility in administering an estate by performing the personal representative's duties. This compensation is for all services performed by the personal representative including distribution of the estate and the conclusion of any trusts. These fees can be varied by the court depending on the complexity of the estate.

The compensation, once determined, must be shared among the personal representatives in the proportions agreed to or as ordered by the court. The following factors are relevant when determining the compensation paid to personal representatives:

(a) the gross value of the estate,

(b) the amount of revenue and disbursements,

(c) the amount of skill, labor, responsibility, technological support, and specialized knowledge required,

(d) the time expended,

(e) the number and complexity of tasks delegated to others, and

(f) the number of personal representatives appointed.

If a lawyer or other agent performs some or all of the duties of the personal representative, the amount payable must be reduced commensurately. Table #1 shows suggested fee guidelines for personal representatives.

j. FEES OF LAWYERS

A lawyer may charge fees for both core legal services and non-core legal services in the administration of estates. The lawyer may also charge fees for legal services that involve

TABLE #1
SUGGESTED FEE GUIDELINES
FOR PERSONAL REPRESENTATIVES

Capital	
On the first $250 000 of capital	3% – 5%
On the next $250 000 of capital	2% – 4%
On the balance	½ of 1% – 3%
Revenue	
On revenue receipts	4% – 6%
Care and management	
On the first $250 000 of capital	$3/10 – 6/10$ of 1%
On the next $250 000 of capital	$2/10 – 5/10$ of 1%
On the balance	$1/10 – 4/10$ of 1%

carrying out the personal representative's duties. The lawyer and the personal representative must agree to the categories of service that the lawyer will perform and to an arrangement or amount for each category of fees, disbursements, and other charges. The fees agreed to must cover, up to the time of distribution of the estate —

(a) all the core legal services and/or non-core legal services,

(b) any personal representative's duties required to be performed by the lawyer, and

(c) any other services required to be performed by the lawyer.

The following factors are relevant when determining the fees charged by or allowed to a lawyer:

(a) The complexity of the work involved and whether any difficult questions were raised

(b) The amount of skill, labor, responsibility and specialized knowledge required

70

(c) The lawyer's experience in estate administration

(d) The number and importance of documents prepared or perused

(e) Whether the lawyer performed services away from his or her usual place of business or in unusual circumstances

(f) The value of the estate

(g) The amount of work performed in connection with jointly held or designated assets

(h) The results obtained

(i) Whether or not the lawyer and the personal representative concluded an agreement and whether the agreement is reasonable in all the circumstances

The lawyer must present a written statement of fees, disbursements, and other charges to the personal representative showing the details of the services performed together with a copy of Part 2 of the Surrogate Rules of Court which set out the specifics of lawyers' compensation. If the account is unacceptable, the personal representative may have the lawyer's account reviewed by a taxing officer of the court. In Part 2 of the Surrogate Court rules, there are tables listing the core legal services and non-core legal services, which you can refer to if necessary. There is also a suggested fee guideline for lawyers to follow. (See Table #2.)

k. READILY AVAILABLE MONEY

As mentioned previously, when death occurs the estate of the deceased is frozen until Letters Probate are issued. This may take several months.

Often, however, a surviving spouse and children require money to live on in the meantime. This may happen in cases where one spouse has not been working and has no immediate source of funds. The law has recognized this need and

TABLE #2
FEE GUIDELINES FOR LAWYERS

Core legal services

Gross value of estate	Base fee	Estate value fee
On estates with a gross value up to $150 000	$2 250	½ of 1%
On estates with a gross value over $150 000	$2 250	1%

Non-core legal services

The fee for non-core legal services is on a *quantum meruit* basis, which means as much as the lawyer charges based on the complexity of the case.

provides certain limited exceptions to the rule that the estate is frozen until the appropriate papers are filed. The more important exceptions are as follows:

(a) Where there is an insurance policy payable to the spouse or anyone else as the beneficiary, the insurance company may pay the amount to the surviving spouse or beneficiary. (In fact, the policy is not part of the estate and the only thing required is the completed claimant form and death certificate.)

(b) Where there is a joint bank account, the entire amount may be withdrawn by the surviving joint holder regardless of whether that person is the spouse or not.

(c) Where the assets of the estate include one or more bank accounts (not joint) or other amounts on deposit, if the deceased person was domiciled in Alberta, any branch of any bank, trust company, or credit union may pay up to $5 000 out of an account without court approval. The financial institution will require completion of its own forms.

(d) Funeral expenses may also be paid out of a bank account with no court approval.

(e) The Bank of Canada will cash Canada Savings Bonds to a value of $8 000 or less, providing the proper indemnity forms are completed.

To obtain any one or more of the above payments, certain documents will be demanded by the individual or company being asked to pay out the money. The person seeking the payment must establish his or her entitlement to the money. Only the formal court papers are not required.

The documents and evidence required in each case vary and no attempt is made here to provide a comprehensive list of the documents needed in every case. If you are involved in a situation where you are attempting to obtain one of these payments, write or telephone the particular institution and ask what their requirements are.

The types of documentation that will likely be requested include items such as the insurance policy, a death certificate, a notarial copy of the will to establish the personal representative's status, a marriage certificate (if the claim is made as a spouse), and any other proof of identity of the claimant that might be requested.

l. FOREIGN DEATH DUTIES

If the deceased owned assets located outside of Alberta, the personal representative will probably be required to file a death tax return in another province or country.

Many foreign countries and states impose death taxes of their own. If a deceased owned property in Florida, for example, while the rest of the assets were located in Alberta, the personal representative will be involved in the filing of a Florida death tax return. Since the laws and the basis of the tax differ, the services of experienced legal counsel in such cases is indispensable.

Sample forms for a basic probate application in Alberta are reproduced in Samples #11 through #22. For a full description of how to file these forms, and for samples of other forms that may be needed in other situations, see *Probate Guide for Alberta*.

SAMPLE #11
APPLICATION BY A PERSONAL REPRESENTATIVE
FOR A GRANT OF PROBATE — FORM NC1

NC 1

COURT FILE NUMBER

COURT   Surrogate Court of Alberta

JUDICIAL DISTRICT   Calgary

ESTATE NAME   James Kamper

PROCEDURE   Application by the personal representative(s) for a Grant of Probate

BOND   Not Required

NOTICES REQUIRED   NC 19 - Notice to Beneficiaries (residuary)
NC 20 - Notice to Beneficiaries (non-residuary)
NC 22 - Notice to Spouse of Deceased (Matrimonial Property Act)
NC 23 - Notice to Spouse of Deceased (Family Relief Act)
NC 24.1 - Notice to Public Trustee

COPY OF THE APPLICATION FILED WITH THE PUBLIC TRUSTEE'S OFFICE   Yes

PERSONAL REPRESENTATIVE(S) NAME(S)   Robert Kamper

COMPLETE ADDRESS FOR SERVICE ON THE PERSONAL REPRESENTATIVE(S)   801 Riverbend Road S.E.
Calgary, Alberta   T2X 1P2

Robert Kamper   *July 25, 199-*

Personal Representative   Date

Name: Robert Kamper
Complete address: 801 Riverbend Road S.E.
Calgary, Alberta   T2X 1P2

SCP-P-ALTA (1-1)96

75

SAMPLE #11 — Continued

NC 1

_____

Lawyers for Personal Representative(s)
Responsible lawyer:
Firm name:
Complete address:

Phone:
Fax:
File No.:

ORDER: ISSUE THE GRANT AS APPLIED FOR

_____   _____

JUDGE OF THE SURROGATE   DATE
COURT OF ALBERTA

_____ certified copies required.

SCP-P-ALTA (1-2)96

SAMPLE #12
AFFIDAVIT BY A PERSONAL REPRESENTATIVE ON APPLICATION FOR A GRANT OF PROBATE — FORM NC2

NC 2

COURT FILE NUMBER

COURT   **Surrogate Court of Alberta**

JUDICIAL DISTRICT   **Calgary**

ESTATE NAME   **James Kamper**

DOCUMENT   **Affidavit by the personal representative(s) on application for a Grant of Probate**

DEPONENT(S) NAME(S)   **Robert Kamper**

DATE OF AFFIDAVIT   **July 25, 199-**

THE DEPONENT SWEARS UNDER OATH OR AFFIRM THAT THE INFORMATION IN THIS AFFIDAVIT AND IN THE ATTACHED SCHEDULES IS WITHIN THE DEPONENTS' KNOWLEDGE AND IS TRUE. WHERE THE INFORMATION IS BASED ON ADVICE OR INFORMATION AND BELIEF, THIS IS STATED.

Applicant

1. The applicant is entitled to apply for a grant because the applicant is the personal representative named in the deceased's last will.

Schedules

2. The following schedules are part of this affidavit. They are correct to the deponent's information and belief.

NC 3	Schedule 1	Deceased
NC 4	Schedule 2	Will
NC 5	Schedule 3	Personal representative(s)
NC 6	Schedule 4	Beneficiaries
NC 7	Schedule 5	Inventory

SCP-P-ALTA (2-1)96

NC 2

Documents

3. The following documents are part of this affidavit.

                                     Original will of the deceased
        NC 8   Affidavit of witness to a will

The schedules and documents that are part of this affidavit provide all the information required in this application by the Surrogate Rules and have been prepared by me or by my lawyer on my behalf.

Notices

4. The applicant(s) have served the following notices as required and in the manner prescribed by the Surrogate Rules.

NC 19	Notice(s) to beneficiaries (residuary)
NC 20	Notice(s) to beneficiaries (non-residuary)
NC 22	Notice to spouse of deceased (Matrimonial Property Act)
NC 23	Notice to spouse of deceased (Family Relief Act)
NC 24.1	Notice to Public Trustee

5. The personal representative(s) will faithfully administer the estate of the deceased according to the law and will give a true accounting of their administration to the persons entitled to it when lawfully required.

SWORN OR AFFIRMED BY EACH DEPONENT BEFORE A COMMISSIONER FOR OATHS AT CALGARY, ALBERTA ON JULY 25, 199-.

_____   _____

Deponent   Commissioner's Name:

                                         Appointment Expiry Date:

SCP-P-ALTA (2-2)96

NC 3

ESTATE NAME   **James Kamper**

DOCUMENT   **Schedule 1: Deceased**

Name   James Kamper

And any other name(s)   N/A
by which known

Last residence address in full   1505 - 14th Street N.W.
                                   Calgary, Alberta T2N 4G2

Date of birth   December 10, 1950

Place of birth   Edmonton, Alberta

Date of death   May 31, 1995

Place of death   Calgary, Alberta

Habitual province/state   Alberta

The deceased died   Testate

IMMEDIATE FAMILY

All immediate family are over 18 and physically and mentally competent unless otherwise shown.

SPOUSE

Name: Stacey Rose Kamper

Complete address: 1505 - 14th Street N.W.
                     Calgary, Alberta T2N 4G2

SCP-P-ALTA (3-1)96

SAMPLE #13 — Continued

CHILDREN

Name:	Kelsey Kamper
Complete address:	1505 - 14th Street N.W.
	Calgary, Alberta T2N 4G2
Age:	1 year
Date of birth:	April 17, 199-
Date of death:	N/A
Died leaving children:	N/A

Name:	Kevin Kamper
Complete address:	123 Centre Street North
	Calgary, Alberta T2X 1Z2
Age:	25 years
Date of birth:	March 1, 19--
Date of death:	N/A
Died leaving children:	N/A

Name:	Karen Kamper
Complete address:	123 Centre Street North
	Calgary, Alberta T2X 1Z2
Age:	22 years
Date of birth:	February 1, 19--
Date of death:	N/A
Died leaving children:	N/A

FORMER SPOUSES

Name:	Kelly Kamper
Complete address:	123 Centre Street North
	Calgary, Alberta T2X 1Z2
Date of death:	N/A
Date of divorce:	March 2, 1985

SCP-P-ALTA (3-2)96

80

SAMPLE #14
SCHEDULE 2: WILL — FORM NC4

NC 4

ESTATE NAME | James Kamper

DOCUMENT | Schedule 2: Will

Date of will | April 20, 1994

Deceased's age at date of will | 39

Marriages of deceased
subsequent to date of will | None

Name of first witness | Joseph Smith

Name of second witness | Sally Red

Neither witness is a beneficiary or the husband or wife of a beneficiary named in the will.

To the best of the personal representative(s) information and belief, this is the deceased's original last will.

The personal representative(s) have examined the will and observe that there appears to be no erasures, changes, or other additions to the will.

SCP-P-ALTA (4-1)96

81

SAMPLE #15
AFFIDAVIT OF WITNESS TO A WILL — FORM NC8

NC 8

TESTATOR NAME	James Kamper
DOCUMENT	Affidavit of witness to will
DEPONENT'S NAME	Joseph Smith
DATE OF AFFIDAVIT	July 24, 1995
EXHIBIT ATTACHED	A: Original will dated April 20, 1994

THE DEPONENT SWEARS UNDER OATH OR AFFIRMS THAT THE INFORMATION IN THIS AFFIDAVIT IS WITHIN THE DEPONENT'S KNOWLEDGE AND IS TRUE. WHERE THE INFORMATION IS BASED ON ADVICE OR INFORMATION AND BELIEF, THIS IS STATED.

1. I am one of the subscribing witnesses to the last will of the deceased, James Kamper.

2. The will is dated April 20, 1994 and is marked as Exhibit A to this affidavit.

3. When the deceased signed the will, I believe the deceased
    3.1 was 18 years of age or more,
    3.2 understood that the document being signed was the deceased's will,
    3.3 was competent to sign the will.

4. The deceased, myself, and the other witness to the will, Sally Red, were all present together when the witnesses and the deceased signed the will.

5. Before the deceased signed the will, the deceased made the following changes to it:
    5.1 N/A

SWORN OR AFFIRMED BEFORE A COMMISSIONER FOR OATHS AT CALGARY, ALBERTA ON JULY 24, 1995.

Joseph Smith
Deponent

I. M. Commissioner
Commissioner's Name: I.M. Commissioner
Appointment Expiry Date: March 31, 199-

SCP-P-ALTA(8-1)96

SAMPLE #16
SCHEDULE 3: PARTICULARS OF THE PERSONAL REPRESENTATIVE(S) — FORM NC5

NC 5

ESTATE NAME   James Kamper

DOCUMENT   Schedule 3: Personal representative(s)

Name(s)   Robert Kamper

Complete address(es)   801 Riverbend Road S.E., Calgary, Alberta, T2X 1P2

Status   Personal representative named in the will

Relationship to deceased   Brother

Age   Over 18

Any persons with a prior or
equal right to apply

Renunciations attached

SCP-P-ALTA (5-1)96

SAMPLE #17
SCHEDULE 4: PARTICULARS OF BENEFICIARIES — FORM NC6

NC 6

ESTATE NAME	James Kamper
DOCUMENT	Schedule 4: Beneficiaries

Name:	Kevin Kamper
Relationship:	Son
Complete address:	123 Centre Street North Calgary, Alberta, T2X 1Z2
Age:	25
Nature of gift:	$100,000.00
Paragraph number of will:	3(c)
Section no. (intestacy):	N/A

Name:	Karen Kamper
Relationship:	Daughter
Complete address:	123 Centre Street North Calgary, Alberta, T2X 1Z2
Age:	22
Nature of gift:	$100,000.00
Paragraph number of will:	3(d)
Section no. (intestacy):	N/A

SCP-P-ALTA (6-1)96

NC 6

Name:	Canadian Cancer Society
Relationship:	None
Complete address:	211, 1301 - 11th Avenue S.W. Calgary, Alberta T2B 1N1
Nature of gift:	$10,000.00
Paragraph number of will:	3(e)
Section no. (intestacy):	N/A

Name:	Stacey Rose Kamper
Relationship:	wife
Complete address:	1505 - 14th Street N.W. Calgary, Alberta T2N 4G2
Age:	30
Nature of gift:	Residue
Paragraph number of will:	3(f)
Section no. (intestacy):	N/A

The following gifts are void because the beneficiary is a witness or the spouse of a witness to the will:

SCP-P-ALTA (6-2)96

85

SAMPLE #18
SCHEDULE 5: INVENTORY OF PROPERTY
AND DEBTS — FORM NC7

NC 7

ESTATE NAME   James Kamper
DOCUMENT   Schedule 5: Inventory of property and debts

VALUE OF ESTATE IN ALBERTA

Land and buildings (net of encumbrances)		$150,000.00
Other property (gross)		$4,182,535.25
Gross value of estate		$4,332,535.25
Debts (excluding encumbrances on land)	$1,207,125.00	
Net value of estate		$3,125,410.25

SUMMARY

Land, mines & minerals, and leasehold interests	$150,000.00
Money or debts due the deceased and secured by a mortgage or agreement for sale	NIL
Cash	$588,435.25
Shares in public and private companies	$3,563,500.00
Bonds, debentures, and treasury bills	$10,600.00
Life insurance payable to the estate	NIL
Annuities, pensions, and benefit plans	NIL
Household goods, personal effects, collections, vehicles, and boats	$20,000.00
Business interests	NIL
Farming interests	NIL
Any other property	NIL

SCP-P-ALTA (7-1)96

SAMPLE #18 — Continued

P R O P E R T Y

LAND AND BUILDINGS

Description:	Condo Plan 921 1123, Unit 6	
Gross value:	$150,000.00	
Encumbrances:	NIL	
Net value:		$150,000.00

OTHER PROPERTY

Description:	Bank of Montreal, Main Branch, Calgary, GIC ($500,000.00) Interest to date of death - $2,000.00	
Gross value:		$502,000.00
Description:	Bank of Montreal, Main Branch, Calgary, Savings Account #215 ($60,000.00) Interest to date of death - $925.25	
Gross value:		$60,925.25
Description:	Bank of Montreal, Main Branch, Calgary, Chequing Account #1112	
Gross value:		$25,510.00
Description:	Canada Savings Bonds ($10,000.00) Interest to date of death - $600.00	
Gross value:		$10,600.00
Description:	2,000,000 shares in Kamper Oil Company Common shares at $1.75/share	
Gross value:		$3,500,000.00
Description:	2,000 shares in Suncor Inc. Common shares at $31.75/share	
Gross value:		$63,500.00
Description:	1994 Jeep	
Gross Value:		$20,000.00

TOTAL VALUE OF PROPERTY   **$4,332,535.25**

SCP-P-ALTA (7-2)96

SAMPLE #18 — Continued

DEBTS

Description: Bank of Montreal, Main Branch, Calgary - term loan
Value: $1,200,000.00

Description: Bank of Montreal VISA
Value: $2,125.00

Description: Jacques Funeral Home
Value: $5,000.00

TOTAL VALUE OF DEBTS   **$1,207,125.00**

NET VALUE OF ESTATE   **$3,125,410.25**

SCP-P-ALTA (7-3)96

SAMPLE #19
NOTICE TO BENEFICIARIES (RESIDUARY) —
FORM NC19

ESTATE NAME   James Kamper

DOCUMENT   Notice to beneficiaries (residuary)

To: Name: Stacey Rose Kamper

    Complete Address: 1505 - 14th Street N.W., Calgary, Alberta, T2N 4G2

You are named as a residuary beneficiary in the last will of James Kamper.

The will gives you the entire residue of the estate.

The personal representative(s) named in the will have applied for a grant of probate.

Enclosed with this notice is a copy of the application for a grant of probate. This includes a copy of the will and a list of the estate property and debts.

Once the court issues the grant, the personal representative(s) will collect the property, pay the debts, and complete the administration of the estate and anything else required of the personal representative(s). Then they will be in a position to account to you before distributing any estate left after payment of all debts and expenses.

You can contact Robert Kamper at 801 Riverbend Road S.E., Calgary, Alberta, T2K 1P2, phone 555-0687, for any further information you may need.

Robert Kamper   *May 15, 199—*
Personal Representative   Date
Name: Robert Kamper
Complete address: 801 Riverbend Road S.E.
                 Calgary, Alberta T2X 1P2

SCP-P-ALTA (13-1)96

SAMPLE #20
AFFIDAVIT OF SERVICE — FORM NC27

COURT FILE NUMBER
ESTATE NAME   James Kamper
DOCUMENT   Affidavit of Service
DEPONENT'S NAME   Robert Kamper
DATE OF AFFIDAVIT   July 25, 1995

THE DEPONENT SWEARS UNDER OATH OR AFFIRMS THAT THE INFORMATION IN
THIS AFFIDAVIT IS WITHIN THE DEPONENT'S KNOWLEDGE AND IS TRUE. WHERE
THE INFORMATION IS BASED ON ADVICE OR INFORMATION AND BELIEF, THIS IS
STATED.

1. On July 24, 1995 I served true copies of the originals of the
    following documents:

Attached as Exhibit	Document
A	Notice to beneficiaries (residuary)
B	Notice to beneficiaries (non-residuary)
C	Notice to beneficiaries (non-residuary)
D	Notice to beneficiaries (non-residuary)
E	Notice to spouse (Family Relief Act)
F	Notice to Public Trustee
G	Notice to spouse (Matrimonial Property Act)

    on the following:

    Person(s) name(s) and address(es) where served and manner of service

1	Stacey Rose Kamper, 1505 - 14th Street N.W., Calgary, Alberta - single registered mail
2	Kevin Kamper, 123 Centre Street North, Calgary, Alberta - single registered mail
3	Karen Kamper, 123 Centre Street North, Calgary, Alberta - single registered mail
4	Canadian Cancer Society, 211, 1301 - 11th Ave. S.W., Calgary Alberta - single registered mail
5	Stacey Rose Kamper, 1505 - 14th Street N.W., Calgary, Alberta - single registered mail
6	Public Trustee, 602 - 7th Ave. S.W., Calgary Alberta - single registered mail

    SCP-P-ALTA (18-1)96

90

SAMPLE #20 — Continued

NC 27

SWORN OR AFFIRMED BY EACH DEPONENT BEFORE A COMMISSIONER
FOR OATHS AT CALGARY, ALBERTA ON JULY 25, 1995.

Robert Kamper

Deponent

Name: Robert Kamper

Complete address: 801 Riverbend Road S.E.
Calgary, Alberta T2X 1P2

Occupation:

Peggy Storey

Commissioner's Name: Peggy Storey

Appointment Expiry Date: March 31, 1997

SCP-P-ALTA (18-2)96

SAMPLE #21
TRANSFER OF LAND

TRANSFER OF LAND

I, FERN GREEN, Personal Representative of the estate of George Green, being registered owner of an estate in fee simple subject to registered encumbrances, liens and interests, if any, in all that piece of land described as follows:

>Lot 10
>Block 1
>Plan 831178

do hereby, in consideration of the sum of One Hundred Twenty Thousand ($120,000.00) Dollars to be paid to me by

BERTHA JONES of 175 Calgary Trail, Edmonton, Alberta, T2X 1Y2

hereinafter called the "Transferee," transfer to the said Transferee all my estate and interest in that piece of land.

IN WITNESS WHEREOF I have hereunto subscribed my name this 24th day of August, 199- .

Signed by the said FERN GREEN)
in the presence of Sally Silver) *Fern Green*
) **FERN GREEN**
)
Sally Silver)
Sally Silver

CONSENT OF SPOUSE

I, FERN GREEN, being married to the deceased, GEORGE GREEN, do hereby give my consent to the disposition of our homestead, made in the attached and I have executed this document for the purpose of giving up my life estate and other dower rights in the said property given to me by the *DOWER ACT*, to the extent necessary to give effect to the said disposition.

Fern Green
FERN GREEN

SCP-P-ALTA(25-1)96

92

CERTIFICATE OF ACKNOWLEDGMENT BY SPOUSE

1.   This document was acknowledged before me by FERN GREEN apart from her husband, her husband having died July 10, 199-

2.   FERN GREEN acknowledged to me that she:
   (a)   is aware of the nature of this disposition;
   (b)   is aware that the *Dower Act*, gives her a life estate in the homestead and the right to prevent disposition of the homestead by withholding consent;
   (c)   consents to the disposition for the purpose of giving up the life estate and other dower rights in the homestead given to her by the *Dower Act*, to the extent necessary to give effect to the said disposition;
   (d)   is executing the document freely and voluntarily without any compulsion on the part of her husband.

   Dated at the City of Edmonton, in the Province of Alberta, this 24th day of August, 1995.

Sally Silver
_____
A COMMISSIONER FOR OATHS IN AND
FOR THE PROVINCE OF ALBERTA
Sally Silver
Commission Expires: January 2, 199-.

SCP-P-ALTA(25-2)96

AFFIDAVIT OF EXECUTION FOR WITNESS

CANADA	)	I, SALLY SILVER
PROVINCE OF ALBERTA	)	of the City of Edmonton,
TO WIT:	)	in the Province of Alberta
	)	MAKE OATH AND SAY:

1. I was personally present and did see FERN GREEN, named in the attached instrument, who is personally known to me to be the person named therein, duly sign and execute the same for the purpose named therein.

2. That the same was executed at Edmonton, in the Province of Alberta on the 24th day of August, 199- and that I am the subscribing witness thereto.

3. That I know the said person and she is, in my belief, of the full age of eighteen years.

SWORN BEFORE ME at the City of   )
Edmonton, in the Province of Alberta,   )
this 24th day of August, 199-.   )
)
)
Isabel Mickey   )
A COMMISSIONER FOR OATHS   )
in and for the Province of Alberta   )
Isabel Mickey
Commission Expires: February 1, 199-.

Sally Silver
SALLY SILVER

SCP-P-ALTA(25-3)96

AFFIDAVIT RE VALUE OF LAND

CANADA	)	I, BERTHA JONES,
PROVINCE OF ALBERTA	)	of the City of Edmonton,
TO WIT:	)	in the Province of Alberta
		MAKE OATH AND SAY:

1.   I am one of the Transferee(s) named in the within or annexed transfer and I know the lands therein described.

2.   I know the circumstances of the Transfer and true consideration to be paid by me is, when completed, as follows:

One Hundred Twenty Thousand ($120,000.00) Dollars, in cash

3.   The Transferor named in the Transfer is the person from whom I acquired the land.

4.   The present value of the land, in my opinion, is $120,000.00 ("land" includes buildings and all other improvements affixed to the land.)

SWORN BEFORE ME at the City of	)
Edmonton, in the Province of Alberta,	)
this 24th day of August, 199-	)
	)
	)
Albert Evans	) *Bertha Jones*
	) BERTHA JONES
A COMMISSIONER FOR OATHS	)
in and for the Province of Alberta	)
Albert Evans	
Commission Expires: September 29, 199-	

SCP-P-ALTA(25-4)96

CERTIFICATE

I, FERN GREEN, the Executrix of the Estate of George Green, certify that George Green was a resident of Canada for all purposes arising under the Income Tax Act of Canada including, but not limited to, Section 116(5) thereof.

Dated this 24th day of August, 199-

Fern Green

FERN GREEN

SCP-P-ALTA(25-5)96

SAMPLE #22
APPLICATION FOR TRANSMISSION

CANADA   )   IN THE MATTER OF THE ESTATE OF THE
PROVINCE OF ALBERTA)   *LAND TITLES ACT* AND IN THE MATTER OF
TO WIT:)   GEORGE GREEN, LATE OF THE CITY OF
)   EDMONTON, IN THE PROVINCE OF
)   ALBERTA, DECEASED

APPLICATION FOR TRANSMISSION

APPLICATION is hereby made for Transmission to Fern Green of 1624 Long Street, in the City of Edmonton, in the Province of Alberta, Personal Representative of the Estate of George Green, late of the City of Edmonton, in the Province of Alberta, Deceased, of the interest of the Deceased in the following lands, namely:

LOT 1
BLOCK 1
PLAN 871 J.K.

PRODUCED herewith is a certified copy of the Grant of Probate with Will annexed of all and singular the property of the said deceased, issued out of the Surrogate Court of Alberta, Judicial District of Edmonton, on the 7th day of August, 199- . pursuant to the fiat of His Honour Judge H.S. Jones wherein the administration of the Estate of the said deceased was granted by the aforesaid Court to the said Fern Green as Executrix.

DATED at the City of Edmonton, in the Province of Alberta, this 7th day of August, 199- .

Fern Green
_____
Fern Green
Applicant

4
ADMINISTRATION

a. WHAT IS AN ADMINISTRATOR?

Chapter 3 dealt with the appointment of a personal representative and the issue of Letters Probate by the Surrogate Court. If an individual dies intestate (i.e., without a will), it is necessary to apply to the Surrogate Court for the appointment of an administrator, who will then proceed to distribute the estate to the heirs-at-law in accordance with the provisions in the Intestate Succession Act. This act also governs the situation where an existing will is invalid, where a will gives no direction as to how part of the estate is to be distributed, or where the will fails to appoint a personal representative.

An administrator is appointed by the court upon the application of one of the heirs of the deceased person. The general rule is that the closest *relative* (not friend) to the deceased has the greatest right to be appointed administrator or administratrix, with the result that should more than one application be made to the court the nearest relative will generally be appointed to the position. Joint applications are possible so that two or more people may be appointed to administer the estate.

Preference must be given to an applicant for a Grant of Administration in the following order, unless the court orders otherwise:

(a) The spouse of the deceased

(b) The child of the deceased

(c) The grandchild of the deceased

(d) Issue of the deceased other than a child or grandchild

(e) Parent of the deceased

(f) Brother or sister of the deceased

(g) Child of the deceased's brother or sister if the child is an heir on intestacy

(h) Next-of-kin of the deceased of closest and equal degree of consanguinity who are heirs on intestacy and who are not otherwise referred to above

(i) Person who has an interest in the estate because of a relationship with the deceased

(j) A claimant

(k) The Crown

If no one applies to be appointed administrator, a legal officer known as the Public Trustee has the right to become the administrator under provincial law. Refer to section **e.** below and Sample #23 for an explanation of priority of the heirs-at-law.

When applying for appointment as an administrator, the same rules apply for the posting of a bond as for an application for probate (see chapter 3).

The application made to the Surrogate Court is for "Letters of Administration" instead of Letters of Probate. (See Samples #23 and #24 for the basic application. For a full discussion of administration, see *Probate Guide for Alberta*.)

b. ADMINISTRATION WITH WILL ANNEXED

Frequently a deceased person will leave a will in which no personal representative is named, or the person named is dead or otherwise incapable of performing the duties required of him or her. Remember that there is no compulsion on anyone to act, even though he or she is named as a personal representative in the will. People refusing to act are said to "renounce" their right to apply for probate.

SAMPLE #23
DIVISION OF AN ESTATE

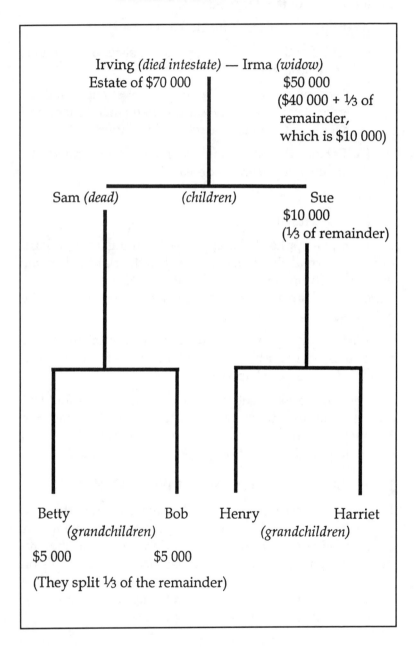

Irving *(died intestate)* — Irma *(widow)*
Estate of $70 000 | $50 000
($40 000 + ⅓ of
remainder,
which is $10 000)

Sam *(dead)* | *(children)* | Sue
$10 000
(⅓ of remainder)

Betty | Bob | Henry | Harriet
(grandchildren) | | *(grandchildren)*
$5 000 | $5 000

(They split ⅓ of the remainder)

SAMPLE #24
APPLICATION FOR GRANT OF ADMINISTRATION —
FORM NC1

NC 1

COURT FILE NUMBER

COURT   Surrogate Court of Alberta

JUDICIAL DISTRICT   Calgary

ESTATE NAME   Dennis Slack

PROCEDURE   APPLICATION BY THE PERSONAL
                                        REPRESENTATIVE FOR
                                        A GRANT OF ADMINISTRATION

BOND   Not required

NOTICES REQUIRED   NC 21 - Notice to beneficiary (intestacy)

                                        NC 24 - Notice to Dependent Child
                                              (Family Relief Act)

COPY OF THE APPLICATION   No
FILED WITH THE PUBLIC
TRUSTEE'S OFFICE

PERSONAL REPRESENTATIVE(S)
NAME(S)   David Slack

COMPLETE ADDRESS FOR   P.O. Box 21,
SERVICE ON THE PERSONAL   Cochrane, Alberta   T0L 0T0
REPRESENTATIVE(S)

David Slack
_____   ___July 25, 199-___
Personal Representative   *Date*
Name: David Slack
Complete address: P.O. Box 21,
                     Cochrane, Alberta   T0L 0T0

SCP-P-ALTA(1-1)96

101

NC 1

Lawyers for Personal Representative(s)
Responsible lawyer:
Firm name:
Complete address:

Phone:
Fax:
File No.:

ORDER: ISSUE THE GRANT AS APPLIED FOR

_____   _____
JUDGE OF THE SURROGATE   DATE
COURT OF ALBERTA

_____ certified copies required

SCP-P-ALTA(1-2)96

SAMPLE #25
AFFIDAVIT BY PERSONAL REPRESENTATIVE ON APPLICATION FOR GRANT OF ADMINISTRATION

NC 2

COURT FILE NUMBER

COURT   **Surrogate Court of Alberta**

JUDICIAL DISTRICT   **Calgary**

ESTATE NAME   **Dennis Slack**

DOCUMENT   **AFFIDAVIT BY THE PERSONAL REPRESENTATIVE(S)**

DEPONENT(S) NAME(S) **David Slack**

DATE OF AFFIDAVIT   **August 24, 199-**

THE DEPONENT SWEARS UNDER OATH OR AFFIRM THAT THE INFORMATION IN THIS AFFIDAVIT AND IN THE ATTACHED SCHEDULES IS WITHIN THE DEPONENT'S KNOWLEDGE AND IS TRUE. WHERE THE INFORMATION IS BASED ON ADVICE OR INFORMATION AND BELIEF, THIS IS STATED.

Applicant

1. The applicant is entitled to apply for a grant because the applicant is the son of the deceased Dennis Slack. The daughter of the deceased, Denise Slack, and the guardian of the son, Darcy Slack, have renounced their right to make an application for a grant.

Schedules

2. The following schedules are part of this affidavit. They are correct to the deponent's information and belief.

2.1	NC 3	Schedule 1	Deceased
2.3	NC 5	Schedule 3	Personal Representative(s)
2.4	NC 6	Schedule 4	Beneficiaries
2.5	NC 7	Schedule 5	Inventory

SCP-P-ALTA(2-1)96

SAMPLE #25 — Continued

NC 2

Documents

3. The schedules and documents that are part of this affidavit provide all the information required in this application by the Surrogate Rules and have been prepared by me or by my lawyer on my behalf.

Notices

4. The applicant(s) have served the following notices as required and in the manner prescribed by the Surrogate Rules.

   4.3   NC 21 Notice to beneficiary (intestate)

   4.6   NC 24 Notice to dependent child of the deceased (Family Relief Act)

5. The personal representative(s) will faithfully administer the estate of the deceased according to the law and will give a true accounting of their administration to the persons entitled to it when lawfully required.

SWORN OR AFFIRMED BY EACH DEPONENT BEFORE A COMMISSIONER FOR OATHS AT _____Calgary___, ALBERTA ON___August 24__, 199-.

David Mack
Deponent

I.M. Commissioner
Commissioner's Name: I.M. Commissioner
Appointment Expiry Date: December 31, 199-

SCP-P-ALTA(2-2)96

A renunciation by a personal representative in no way invalidates the will. It continues to govern the disposition of the deceased's assets. However, as no one named in the will is available to carry out its provisions, the court will have to appoint an administrator. Usually the closest relative to the deceased will make the necessary application to the Surrogate Court for what are known as Letters of Administration With Will Annexed. (See Sample #26 and the *Probate Guide* for a full explanation of this procedure.) This is a court document that appoints an administrator whose job it is to distribute the assets of the estate in accordance with the provisions of the will.

c. WHAT IS A PUBLIC TRUSTEE?

In cases where there is no will and no one steps forward to act as administrator or where there is a will and no one is willing to act, the estate comes under the jurisdiction of a provincial government office called the Public Trustee's Office.

The lack of an administrator happens quite frequently because there are an amazing number of people who have no wills and no known living relatives. Also, in cases of multiple disasters, children are often left without relatives to look after the financial affairs of their parents' estate.

The Public Trustee's Office is very busy, so lengthy delays may occur whenever it becomes responsible for administering an estate.

d. COMMON-LAW MARRIAGES AND ADMINISTRATION

At the outset we should point out that the law recognizes common-law marriages only in a few limited cases, and even in these cases there are always procedural difficulties involved in enforcing your rights. Therefore, it is doubly important in this situation that you have a will.

At present, if there is no will, the common-law spouse is not recognized in Alberta. This means that even though a

SAMPLE #26
APPLICATION FOR GRANT OF ADMINISTRATION
WITH WILL ANNEXED — FORM NC1

NC 1

COURT FILE NUMBER

COURT   **Surrogate Court of Alberta**

JUDICIAL DISTRICT   **Drumheller**

ESTATE NAME   **John Jones**

PROCEDURE   **APPLICATION BY THE PERSONAL REPRESENTATIVE FOR A GRANT OF ADMINISTRATION WITH WILL ANNEXED**

BOND   **Not required**

NOTICES REQUIRED   **NC 19 - Notice to beneficiary (residuary)**

COPY OF THE APPLICATION   **Yes**
FILED WITH THE PUBLIC
TRUSTEE'S OFFICE

PERSONAL REPRESENTATIVE(S)
NAME(S)   **Denise Doe**

COMPLETE ADDRESS FOR   **555 Fly By Way,**
SERVICE ON THE PERSONAL   **Drumheller, Alberta Z1P 0G0**
REPRESENTATIVE(S)

Denise Doe   _July 25, 199—_
Personal Representative   Date
Name: Denise Doe
Complete address: 555 Fly By Way,
                      Drumheller, Alberta Z1P 0G0

SCP-P-ALTA(1-1-)96

NC 1

Lawyers for Personal Representative(s)
Responsible lawyer:
Firm name:
Complete address:

Phone:
Fax:
File No.:

ORDER: ISSUE THE GRANT AS APPLIED FOR

JUDGE OF THE SURROGATE   DATE
COURT OF ALBERTA

_____ certified copies required

SCP-P-ALTA(1-2)96

couple may have been living together for 20 years and have conducted their affairs as though they were married, when the "husband" dies, the "wife" may have no rights to any part of his estate unless he leaves a valid will. There is no all-encompassing definition of the term "common law spouse." The term has been used to describe people in relationships of various degrees of seriousness and length. The term is not readily found in legislation. Whether a person qualifies as a "spouse" depends on the terms of the relevant legislation and the facts of each relationship.

1. Income Tax Act

A spouse under the Income Tax Act includes a person who has lived in a conjugal relationship with an individual of the opposite sex for a year or more.

2. Canada Pension Plan

If the age and other requirements of the Canada Pension Plan are met, a pension will be payable to the surviving spouse of a deceased contributor. A spouse of a contributor means "a person of the opposite sex who is cohabiting with the contributor in a conjugal relationship at the relevant time, having cohabited with the contributor for a continuous period of at least one year."

3. Family Relief Act

The Family Relief Act allows "dependants" of the deceased to bring an application for maintenance and support from the deccased's estate. "Spouse" is not defined, but has been consistently interpreted to mean a legal spouse. In 1994, the Court of Queen's Bench considered this issue and held that the court had the jurisdiction to include a common law spouse in the definition of spouse. When the Court of Appeal heard the appeal, because the application involved a Charter of Rights argument, the court sent the matter back for a full trial, including the question of the definition of spouse in the Family Relief Act. The matter never went to trial. The current state of the law seems to be that a common law spouse is not entitled to bring an application for maintenance and support unless accompanied by a successful Charter challenge to the legislation.

4. Matrimonial Property Act

Section 1(e) of the Matrimonial Property Act defines "spouse" to include a former spouse and a party to a marriage notwithstanding that the marriage is void or voidable. The definition does not include or exclude common law spouses. However, the context of the entire act suggests that it applies to married spouses or former married spouses, and does not include common law spouses.

5. Intestate Succession Act

Only the survivor of a legally married couple qualifies as a spouse under the Intestate Succession Act. Therefore, a common law spouse of a deceased person who dies without a will cannot advance a claim against the estate. The common law spouse also lacks the status to apply to the appointed personal representative of the estate.

6. Dower Act

The surviving spouse of a deceased is granted a life estate in the household and the real property of the "homestead" of the deceased married person by virtue of the Dower Act. This act refers only to "married people" and does not define "spouse."

7. Domestic Relations Act

A recent Alberta Court of Appeal decision dealing with the Domestic Relations Act held that it is unconstitutional to exclude common law spouses from bringing an application for spousal support. The court gave the Alberta government one year to amend the legislation. The government has not enacted new legislation.

The injustice of this is obvious, and it is hoped that the Alberta government will move, as have other provinces, to correct this situation.

8. Unjust enrichment

The doctrine of unjust enrichment is the remedy most frequently used by common law spouses seeking relief against an estate. Essentially, when a surviving common law spouse makes a claim against the deceased's estate based on unjust enrichment, the claim will be successful where the following three conditions are met:

(a) There is an enrichment to the deceased's estate.

(b) There is a corresponding deprivation to the surviving common law spouse.

(c) There is an absence of any legal reason for the enrichment. The fundamental concern is the legitimate expectation of the parties.

As far as children are concerned, the child of an unmarried woman is recognized as her legitimate child for the purposes of inheritance. The child of an unmarried man will not be entitled to share in his or her father's estate unless either of the following occurs:

(a) The father has acknowledged paternity (this is a question of fact in each case) or

(b) A court order has been made about the father's paternity under any one of the following acts:

  (i) The Child Welfare Act

  (ii) The Parentage and Maintenance Act

Legally adopted children assume all the rights and privileges of a natural child.

e. HOW IS THE ESTATE DIVIDED IF THERE IS NO WILL?

If there is no will, the estate is distributed to family members in accordance with the following chart.

Distribution of Estate in Administration		
Survivors	Value of estate	Beneficiaries and amounts received
(1) Spouse and children	Less than $40 000	Entire estate to spouse
(2) Spouse and children	More than $40 000	Spouse gets $40 000 and — (a) if one child, spouse gets one-half of residue and child gets one-half (b) if more than one child, spouse gets one-third of residue and children split two-thirds of residue
(3) Spouse with no children	Any amount	Spouse
(4) No spouse or issue	Any amount	In equal shares to father and mother, or everything to surviving parent
(5) No spouse, issue, or parent	Any amount	Equally to sisters and brothers; if brother or sister is dead their children will take their share

(6) No spouse, issue, parents, brothers, or sisters	Any amount	Equally to nieces and nephews
(7) No spouse, issue, parents, brothers, sisters, nieces, or nephews	Any amount	Equally among the next-of-kin of equal degree of consanguinity

If there is no spouse of the deceased and no surviving blood relatives, the whole estate will go to the provincial government.

f. EXAMPLES OF ADMINISTRATION

Example 1

If a married man or woman dies without a will leaving no issue, the entire estate goes to the survivor. If both die in an accident, the younger is considered to have survived the elder and consequently, if the wife is in fact younger than her husband, then the estate goes to her relatives.

Example 2

If a widow or widower dies without a will and leaving children, the estate is divided equally among the children.

Example 3

In Sample #23, if Irving died without a will and left an estate of $70 000, and Irving's son Sam is dead, the distribution would be like this:

(a) To Irma, Irving's widow — $40 000 plus $10 000 (⅓ of the remaining $30 000)

(b) To Sue, $10 000 (⅓ of the remaining $30 000)

(c) To Betty and Bob, $5 000 each (sharing ⅓ of the remaining $30 000). (If Betty were dead, Bob would inherit $10 000 (the whole ⅓ of the remainder).)

For a full discussion of administration of an estate where no executor exists, see *Probate Guide for Alberta,* another title in the Self-Counsel Series.

5
TAX CONSIDERATIONS

a. CAPITAL GAINS TAX

A capital gains tax is a tax based on the amount of profit or gain made by a person when he or she disposes of an asset. For example, if Teri Taxpayer bought ten shares of Bell Canada in March, 1999, for $420 (including brokerage charges) and sold those ten shares in August, 1999, for $460 (after deducting brokerage charges), she has made a capital gain of $40.

She must declare this gain in her tax return filed for the year in which the property is sold. The January 1994 Federal Budget removed all capital gains exemptions. If capital property was acquired prior to February 1994, there may be certain exemptions available if the correct documentation is filed with revenue Canada. It is strongly recommended that you seek advice from your tax accountant.

b. CAPITAL GAINS ON DEATH

The significance of the taxation of capital gains for the discussion in this book is that an individual is considered, for the purposes of the Income Tax Act, to have sold all of his or her assets on the day of death for an amount equal to their current "fair market value." Fair market value merely means the value of the item if the owner were to attempt to sell it on the open market.

Though a capital gain is normally only experienced and taxed when an asset is sold or given away, the Income Tax Act provides for the imposition of this tax when the individual dies. This is referred to as a "deemed disposition."

c. FILING THE TAX RETURN

One of the many duties of the personal representative is to file the income tax return for the deceased person for the year of death, along with the other returns not yet filed. The personal representative is allowed six months or until April 30, whichever is the longer period, to file the income tax return for the year of death.

Referring to a hypothetical estate again, if Jane Ellen Angel died on March 1, 1999, she would probably not have filed her 1998 income tax return, which was due April 30, 1999. The personal representative must file the 1998 return by April 30, 1999 or pay late filing charges. The tax return for January and February of 1999 would be filed on or before April, 2000, when the new tax return forms for the year of 1999 become available.

In preparing and filing the deceased's income tax return, the personal representative must declare, and pay tax on, gains on all the assets owned by the deceased on the day of death as though the deceased had sold all assets on that date. Any increase in value over the cost of the assets in the estate will result in a capital gain.

The Income Tax Act provides specifically for an exemption from capital gains tax on death if the property upon which a capital gain has been realized passes to the spouse of the deceased person either under the provisions of a will or on account of the Intestate Succession Act. Thus, there will be no capital gains tax payable on the estate of someone who leaves everything to his or her spouse.

If the estate is left instead to, for example, a brother or anyone other than a spouse, it would be necessary to obtain values for all the assets of the estate and calculate what capital gains and capital losses are involved.

d. TAX CLEARANCE CERTIFICATE

Only after Revenue Canada has issued a clearance certificate can the personal representative be sure that the deceased has no more obligations to the tax department. It is necessary to insure that all required tax returns prior to the date of death be filed, as well as the return for the year of the death. The final T-3 return should be submitted after receipt of the assessment of the year of death return. It is then time to request a clearance certificate for distribution purposes. The request should include the following:

(a) A copy of the assessment of the date of death return

(b) A copy of the will, if one exists

(c) A copy of the Application for Probate or Administration

(d) A copy of any appraisals of estate assets

(e) A copy of any court orders or agreements altering the distribution of the estate

e. WHAT IMPACT THE GST HAS ON ESTATES

The goods and services tax (GST), does not greatly affect the administration of estates, but personal representatives must keep it in mind.

In most cases, GST will not be payable, but if the deceased participated in commercial ventures there may be tax owing. If there is any question about whether any GST is owing, it is advisable to seek professional help who may be able to find ways to minimize the tax. (See Table #3, which provides guidelines for certain types of property.) If GST is involved in the administration of an estate, the personal representative could be held personally liable for its payment. This can be avoided by obtaining a GST clearance certificate.

TABLE #3
PROPERTY TYPE AND GST CONSEQUENCES

Property type	*GST Consequences*
(a) Cash, bonds and debentures, mortgages, guaranteed investment certificates, shares, RRSPs, RSPs, insurance proceeds	Exempt (financial service)
(b) Principal residence, cottage	Exempt (used residential property)
(c) Cars, jewellery, personal effects	Taxable only if distributed in a commercial activity
(d) Commercial real estate	Taxable

6
THE CANADA PENSION PLAN

a. BENEFITS UNDER THE PLAN

Too often people forget Canada Pension Plan benefits that are payable on the death of a deceased contributor. Practically all individuals earning income from employment as well as self-employed individuals must contribute to the plan.

On the death of any individual who has contributed to the plan during a minimum of three calendar years, a total of four possible types of survivor's benefits become available:

(a) A death benefit is payable to the estate in a lump sum. This is to be used to help defray immediate expenses such as funeral and ambulance costs.

(b) The surviving spouse may be entitled to a monthly pension.

(c) The surviving dependent children may be entitled to a monthly pension.

(d) A disabled spouse of a deceased person who can show that he or she relied completely or to a large degree on his or her spouse for maintenance (financial support) may qualify for a monthly pension.

The personal representative and the surviving spouse should carefully consider the potential benefits to see which, if any, are payable in the particular circumstances of the estate with which they are dealing.

b. LUMP-SUM DEATH BENEFIT

A lump-sum death benefit is payable to the estate of a person who contributed to the plan for all or part of four years since the plan began in 1966. The four years do not have to be consecutive but could have been spread out (e.g., there could have been earnings in 1966, 1971, 1977, and 1985).

The size of the lump-sum payment will depend on the amount actually contributed to the plan by the deceased. The amount is calculated on the basis of six times the monthly retirement pension that he or she was collecting. If the deceased was not yet collecting a pension, then a calculation is made to see what the pension would have been at the date of death if he or she had been eligible for a pension on that date. The lump-sum amount will be six times the hypothetical pension. The maximum lump-sum death benefit payment for a death occurring in 1998 is $2 500.

Application forms for the lump-sum death benefit can be obtained free of charge upon request at the local office of the Canada Pension Plan. These are spread throughout the province.

Various documents must accompany the application. These include —

(a) a death certificate,

(b) the deceased's birth certificate, and

(c) the deceased's social insurance card.

An Application for Death Benefit is shown in Sample #27.

The death benefit is the only benefit that is retroactive for more than one year. So, even if the executors or administrators had overlooked this fact five years ago, they could put in an application today.

c. SURVIVORS' PENSION

If the deceased contributor is survived by a spouse, he or she may be eligible for the survivors' pension. It is once again necessary for the deceased person to have contributed to the plan for the minimum contributory period. The precise amount of the pension depends on a number of factors including the amount of actual contributions to the plan, the age of the applicant, and the number of dependent children who survive the deceased. Upon assessing these various factors, a monthly pension is calculated.

Under the Canada Pension Plan, no survivors' pension is payable to a person who was at the time of the death of the contributor under the age of 35 unless he or she had dependent children or is disabled.

Application forms for the survivors' pension can be obtained free of charge from the local office of the Canada Pension Plan (see Sample #28).

Various documents must accompany the application. These include —

(a) a death certificate,

(b) the deceased's birth certificate,

(c) the deceased's social insurance card,

(d) the marriage certificate,

(e) the survivor's birth certificate, and

(f) the survivor's social insurance card.

Four of the required documents duplicate the requirements for the application for a lump-sum death benefit. If both types of benefits are being applied for, it is usual to send in both applications at the same time.

The plan includes regulations regarding the entitlement to a survivor's pension in situations where the spouse remarries or where the husband and wife separated or were divorced prior to the death. If husband and wife are divorced prior to the death of the deceased contributor, the former spouse is not eligible for a survivor's pension at all.

If husband and wife are separated prior to the death of the deceased contributor, the surviving spouse may or may not be entitled to a survivor's pension depending on the circumstances.

d. BENEFITS FOR DEPENDENT CHILDREN

Benefits for dependent children are also payable on the death of a contributor. To be eligible for the benefits payable, the child must be unmarried, the natural or adopted child of the deceased contributor, under the age of 18, or between 18 and 25 if the child attends school or university full-time.

The result of a successful application will be a monthly pension payable to the parent or guardian of the child until he or she is 18. If the pension continues after the age of 18 because the child is in full-time attendance at school or university, it is payable directly to the child. The child's pension continues only as long as he or she meets the qualifications for eligibility stated above.

The application form for the survivors' pension doubles as an application for benefits for dependent children under the age of 18. By filling in additional parts of the form, the two applications are made simultaneously. If application is being made by a child over the age of 18, a separate form is available from the local office of the Canada Pension Plan.

Additional documents that will be required include —

(a) the birth certificate of each child, and

(b) a social insurance card (if any) for each child.

Sample #29 shows a Declaration of Attendance at School or University and Sample #30 shows an Application for Child's Benefit.

e. COMMON-LAW RELATIONSHIPS

If it can be shown that the deceased and the applicant had for a period of at least three years prior to the death resided together and publicly represented themselves as husband and wife, and if they were unable to marry during that period because of a previous marriage of either of them, then the government has the discretion to direct that, for the purposes of the Canada Pension Plan only, the surviving common-law spouse shall be treated as the spouse of the deceased.

Where there was nothing preventing the marriage of the applicant and the deceased and it can be shown that the parties had resided together for a period of at least one year prior to the death and that the applicant had been publicly represented by the deceased as his or her spouse, the same discretion applies.

Accordingly, if such discretion is exercised in favor of a common-law spouse, the normal application can be made by the survivor for the benefits that would have been available under the plan had the survivor and the deceased contributor actually been married.

SAMPLE #27
APPLICATION FOR DEATH BENEFITS

Health and Welfare Canada — Santé et Bien-être social Canada
Income Security Programs — Programmes de la sécurité du revenu

Français au verso

Personal Information
Bank NHW/P-PU-141

FOR PERTINENT INFORMATION WITH RESPECT TO THE PRIVACY ACT, PLEASE SEE INFORMATION SHEET.

APPLICATION
DEATH BENEFIT
CANADA PENSION PLAN

— COMPLETE THE UNSHADED AREAS
— PLEASE PRINT

LANGUAGE PREFERENCE
ENGLISH ☒ FRENCH ☐

SECTION A — INFORMATION ABOUT THE DECEASED CONTRIBUTOR

FOR OFFICE USE ONLY

1A. CONTRIBUTOR'S SOCIAL INSURANCE NUMBER 9 8 7 6 5 4 3 2 1
1B. Male ☒ Female ☐
1C. DATE OF BIRTH Day 10 Month 02 Year 21

AA

2A. MARITAL STATUS Single ☐ Married ☒ Widow(er) ☐ Separated ☐ Divorced ☐ Common-law ☐
2B. DATE OF DEATH Day 15 Month 05 Year 41

DATE OF DEATH ESTABL | PROV. CODE

AA

3. MR., MRS., ETC. GIVEN NAME AND INITIAL GEORGE
FAMILY NAME GREEN

SURNAME — VALIDATOR

AR

4. HOME ADDRESS (Number and Street) 1624 Long Street   (Apt. No., PO Box, R.R. No)

5. (City, Town or Village) Calgary **(Province or Territory)** Alberta **(Country)** Canada **(Postal Code)** 2 1 P 0 G 0

6A. IF ADDRESS ABOVE IS OUTSIDE OF CANADA, INDICATE THE PROVINCE IN WHICH THE DECEASED RESIDED
6B. DECEASED'S LAST NAME AT BIRTH Same as 3 above ☒ or

7A. WAS THE DECEASED EVER IN RECEIPT OF, OR HAD THE DECEASED EVER APPLIED FOR A BENEFIT UNDER: The Canada Pension Plan? Yes ☐ No ☒ | The Quebec Pension Plan? Yes ☐ No ☒ | The Old Age Security Act? Yes ☐ No ☒
7B. IF YES, INDICATE UNDER WHAT SOCIAL INSURANCE NUMBER.

8. HAS THE DECEASED EVER PARTICIPATED IN A SOCIAL INSURANCE PLAN OF ANOTHER COUNTRY? Yes ☐ No ☒ ▶ INDICATE NAME OF COUNTRY(IES) AND INSURANCE NUMBER(S).

9A. IF APPLICABLE, INDICATE SPOUSE'S FULL NAME AND SOCIAL INSURANCE NUMBER, IF AVAILABLE.
FERN B. GREEN   1 0 1 1 2 1 4 2

9B. IS THERE: Yes No
AN EXECUTOR OF THE ESTATE? OR ☒ ☐
AN ADMINISTRATOR OF THE ESTATE? OR ☐ ☐
A LEGAL REPRESENTATIVE OF THE ESTATE? ☐ ☐

A

10. THE ESTATE OF GEORGE GREEN

11. INDICATE COMPLETE NAME OF PERSON OR AGENCY AND ITS REPRESENTATIVE REFERRED TO IN QUESTION 9B. (if applicable)
FERN B. GREEN

B

12. ADDRESS OF PERSON OR AGENCY NAMED IN 11. (Number and Street) 1624 Long Street (Apt. No., PO Box, R.R. No.)
TYPE NM ADR | FOREIGN CODE | LANG

C

13. (City, Town or Village) Calgary **(Province or Territory)** Alberta **(Country)** Canada **(Postal Code)** 2 1 P 0 G 0
CONS. CODE | NO. LNS 2 0 | A L

D

14. DID THE DECEASED OR THE DECEASED'S SPOUSE RECEIVE FAMILY ALLOWANCES SINCE JANUARY 1, 1966, FOR CHILDREN BORN AFTER DECEMBER 31, 1958?
DECEASED CONTRIBUTOR Yes ☒ No ☐ | DECEASED'S SPOUSE Yes ☐ No ☐

SECTION B — INFORMATION ABOUT THE APPLICANT

15A. MR., MRS., ETC. GIVEN NAME AND INITIAL FERN B. **FAMILY NAME** GREEN
15B. RELATIONSHIP OF APPLICANT TO DECEASED WIFE

A

16. FOR THE ESTATE OF GEORGE GREEN **ADDRESS (Number and Street, Apt. No., PO Box, R.R. No.)** 1624 Long Street
TYPE NM ADR | FOREIGN CODE | LANG

B

17. (City, Town or Village) Calgary **(Province or Territory)** Alberta **(Country)** Canada **(Postal Code)** 2 1 P G G 0
CONS. CODE | NO. LNS 2 0 | A L

C

SECTION C — DECLARATION OF THE APPLICANT

18. I hereby apply on behalf of the estate of the deceased contributor for a Death Benefit. I declare that, to the best of my knowledge and belief, the information given in this application is true and complete.

SIGNATURE OF APPLICANT *Fern Green*
DATE OF APPLICATION Day 15 Month 06 Year 9
TELEPHONE NUMBER 123-4567

IT IS AN OFFENCE TO MAKE A FALSE OR MISLEADING STATEMENT IN THIS APPLICATION.

— HWC PROTECTED —

SAMPLE #28
APPLICATION FOR SURVIVORS' BENEFITS

Health and Welfare Canada — Santé et Bien-être social Canada
Income Security Programs — Programmes de la sécurité du revenu

Français au verso
Personal Information
Bans HWH/P-PU-147
FOR PERTINENT INFORMATION WITH RESPECT TO THE PRIVACY ACT, PLEASE SEE INFORMATION SHEET.

APPLICATION
SURVIVORS' BENEFITS
CANADA PENSION PLAN

— COMPLETE THE UNSHADED AREAS
— PLEASE PRINT

LANGUAGE PREFERENCE
ENGLISH ☒   FRENCH ☐

SECTION A — INFORMATION ABOUT THE DECEASED CONTRIBUTOR

		FOR OFFICE USE ONLY
1A. CONTRIBUTOR'S SOCIAL INSURANCE NUMBER 9 8 7 6 5 4 3 2 1	1B. Male ☒ Female ☐ 1C. DATE OF BIRTH Day 1 Month 0 Year 0 2 2 1	AGE ESTABLISHED
2A. MARITAL STATUS Single ☐ Married ☒ Widowers ☐ Divorced ☐ Separated ☐ Common-law ☐	2B. DATE OF DEATH Day 1 Month 5 0 5 Year 9 -	DATE OF DEATH ESTABL PROV CODE
3. MR., MRS., ETC. GIVEN NAME AND INITIAL GEORGE FAMILY NAME GREEN		SURNAME — VALIDATOR
4. HOME ADDRESS (Number and Street) 1624 Long Street	(Apt No., PO Box, R.R. No.)	
5. (City, Town or Village) Calgary (Province or Territory) Alberta (Country) Canada	(Postal Code) 2 1 P 0 G 0	

SECTION B — INFORMATION ABOUT THE SURVIVING SPOUSE

		FOR OFFICE USE ONLY
6A. YOUR SOCIAL INSURANCE NUMBER 1 0 1 1 2 1 1 4 2	6B. Male ☐ Female ☒ 6C. YOUR DATE OF BIRTH Day 1 0 Month 1 2 Year 3 1	AGE ESTABLISHED
7. MR., MRS., ETC. GIVEN NAME AND INITIAL FERN B. FAMILY NAME GREEN		DSB START DSB END
8. HOME ADDRESS (Number and Street) 1624 Long Street	(Apt. No., PO Box, R.R. No.)	TYPE NM ADR FOREIGN CODE LANG
9. (City, Town or Village) Calgary (Province or Territory) Alberta (Country) Canada	(Postal Code) 2 1 P 0 G 0	CONS. CODE NO LNS 2 1 A L
10. MAILING ADDRESS IF DIFFERENT FROM 8 ABOVE (Number and Street)	(Apt. No., PO Box, R.R. No.)	TYPE NM ADR FOREIGN CODE LANG
11. (City, Town or Village) (Province or Territory) (Country)	(Postal Code)	CONS. CODE NO LNS 2 1 A L
12A. IF ADDRESS SHOWN IN 8 ABOVE IS OUTSIDE OF CANADA INDICATE THE LAST PROVINCE OF RESIDENCE.	12B. ARE YOU DISABLED? ☐ Yes ☒ No	
13A. ARE YOU RECEIVING OR HAVE YOU EVER RECEIVED OR APPLIED FOR A BENEFIT UNDER: The Canada Pension Plan? ☐ Yes ☒ No The Quebec Pension Plan? ☐ Yes ☒ No The Old Age Security Act? ☐ Yes ☒ No	13B. If YES, INDICATE UNDER WHAT SOCIAL INSURANCE NUMBER.	
14. YOUR NAME AT BIRTH SAME AS 7 ABOVE ☐ OR FERN B. GROVE		MARRIAGE ESTABLISHED

15A. WERE YOU MARRIED TO THE DECEASED CONTRIBUTOR?	15B. WERE YOU STILL MARRIED AT THE TIME OF THE CONTRIBUTOR'S DEATH? ☒ Yes ☐ No
Yes ☒ Enter date of marriage ▶ Day 28 Month 8 Year 50 /Submit Marriage Certificate	
No ☐ When did you start living together? ▶ Day Month Year	15C. WERE YOU STILL LIVING TOGETHER AT THE TIME OF THE CONTRIBUTOR'S DEATH? ☐ Yes ☐ No

16. IF YOU WERE UNDER 45 YEARS OF AGE AT THE TIME OF THE CONTRIBUTOR'S DEATH, WERE YOU WHOLLY OR SUBSTANTIALLY MAINTAINING

	Yes	No
A. A CHILD OF THE CONTRIBUTOR UNDER 18 YEARS OF AGE WHO WAS NOT IN YOUR CUSTODY AND CONTROL?	☐	☐
B. A DISABLED CHILD OF THE CONTRIBUTOR AGE 18 OR OVER?	☐	☐
C. A CHILD OF THE CONTRIBUTOR AGE 18 TO 25 IN FULL TIME ATTENDANCE AT SCHOOL OR UNIVERSITY?	☐	☐

If yes to any of the above, explain the circumstances on a separate sheet of paper and indicate whether or not the maintenance is continuing.

SECTION C — INFORMATION ABOUT THE CHILDREN WHO ARE UNDER AGE 18

			FOR OFFICE USE ONLY	
17A. SOCIAL INSURANCE NUMBER OF CHILD	17B. Male ☐ Female ☐ 17C. DATE OF BIRTH Day Month Year	AGE ESTABLISHED M Y	CANCELLATION M Y REASON	DA
18. GIVEN NAME OF CHILD INITIAL FAMILY NAME		DPND END M Y DSB START M Y	DSB END M Y A L	DA
19A. SOCIAL INSURANCE NUMBER OF CHILD	19B. Male ☐ Female ☐ 19C. DATE OF BIRTH Day Month Year	AGE ESTABLISHED M Y	CANCELLATION M Y REASON	DB
20. GIVEN NAME OF CHILD INITIAL FAMILY NAME		DPND END M Y DSB START M Y	DSB END M Y A L	DB

LIST ADDITIONAL CHILDREN ON A SEPARATE SHEET OF PAPER AND ATTACH TO THIS APPLICATION

21. ARE ALL OF THE CHILDREN LISTED THE NATURAL OR LEGALLY ADOPTED CHILDREN OF THE CONTRIBUTOR? ☐ Yes ☐ No If no, indicate each child who is not on a separate sheet of paper

124

22.	ARE ANY OF THE CHILDREN LISTED RECEIVING OR HAVE THEY APPLIED FOR BENEFITS UNDER	A. THE CANADA PENSION PLAN? ☐ Yes ☐ No	B. THE QUEBEC PENSION PLAN? ☐ Yes ☐ No	If yes, indicate which children and under which Social Insurance Number on a separate sheet of paper.
23.	ARE ALL OF THE CHILDREN LISTED STILL IN YOUR CUSTODY AND CONTROL?	☐ Yes ☐ No		If no, indicate each child who is not and give the date each child ceased to be in your custody and control on a separate sheet of paper.
24.	HAVE YOU BEEN WHOLLY OR SUBSTANTIALLY MAINTAINING ALL OF THE CHILDREN LISTED SINCE THE DEATH OF THE CONTRIBUTOR?	☐ Yes ☐ No		If no, explain on a separate sheet of paper

SECTION D — INFORMATION ABOUT THE APPLICANT IF OTHER THAN THE SURVIVING SPOUSE NAMED IN SECTION B OR IF SECTION B IS BLANK

25.	MR., MRS., ETC.	GIVEN NAME AND INITIAL	FAMILY NAME			
26.	HOME ADDRESS (Number and Street)		(Apt. No., P.O. Box, R.R. No.)	TYPE NM ADR	FOREIGN CODE	LANG.
27.	(City, Town or Village) (Province or Territory)	(Country)	(Postal Code)	CONS. CODE	NO. LNS	A L.

ATTACH A SEPARATE SHEET OF PAPER EXPLAINING WHY YOU ARE MAKING THIS APPLICATION.

SECTION E — DECLARATION OF THE APPLICANT

28. I declare that, to the best of my knowledge and belief, the information given in this application is true and complete and I undertake to notify the Income Security Programs Branch of any changes in circumstances that may affect eligibility for benefits.

DECLARATION OF WITNESS REQUIRED ONLY WHEN APPLICANT SIGNS BY MARK

I have read the contents of this application to the applicant who appeared fully to understand them and who made his or her mark in my presence.

SIGNATURE OF APPLICANT ▶ *Jem B. Green*

SIGNATURE OF WITNESS

DATE OF APPLICATION
Day | Month | Year
15 | 0 6 | 91 —

Note: Signature by mark (X) is acceptable if witnessed by any responsible person who must complete the declaration opposite.

ADDRESS OF WITNESS

TELEPHONE NUMBER
123 - 4567

TELEPHONE NUMBER

IT IS AN OFFENCE TO MAKE A FALSE OR MISLEADING STATEMENT IN THIS APPLICATION.

OFFICE USE ONLY — DO NOT WRITE BELOW THIS LINE

BENEFIT INFORMATION																		
ACTION	BNFT	AL	B/C	D	E	F	G	S		C.P.P. NUMBER				DT. EFF. D M Y	CHILD M Y SONC			

0.0 — EA

ACCESS CODE		ACTION	BNFT	DT. EFF. M Y	CHILD SONC	MISCELLANEOUS 1 (OLD)	MISCELLANEOUS 2 (NEW)	B/C	D E F G S	NUMBER OF LINES

0,0 0,0 — EC

MONETARY INFO

CODE	CHILD SONC	(RECOVERY) BNFT CHLD	SIGN	UNDER/OVPYMT	ACCRUED RECOVERY CPP	OPP	DT. EFF. M Y	CPP WITHHOLD ARREARS RATE	OPP WITHHOLD ARREARS RATE
										FA
										FA
										FA
TOTAL			▶							FE

EARNINGS

YR	TYPE	PLAN	CATEGORY	EARNINGS	CONTRIBUTIONS	TOTAL EARNINGS	CONTRIBUTIONS	
								GA
							DATE APPLICATION RECEIVED	GA

Application taken by:

Application approved pursuant to Subsection 19(3) of the Canada Pension Plan.   Date

Effective Date   Authorized Signature

	DATE	TYPE OF REJECT	BATCH NO	CYCLE	DATE	SIGNATURE
1						
2						

SAMPLE #29
DECLARATION OF ATTENDANCE
AT SCHOOL OR UNIVERSITY

DECLARATION OF ATTENDANCE AT SCHOOL OR UNIVERSITY
DÉCLARATION DE FRÉQUENTATION SCOLAIRE OU UNIVERSITAIRE

Canada Pension Plan
Régime de pensions du Canada

LANGUAGE PREFERENCE
INDIQUEZ LA LANGUE QUE VOUS PREFEREZ UTILISER

☒ ENGLISH / ANGLAIS   ☐ FRENCH / FRANÇAIS

SECTION A — TO BE COMPLETED BY STUDENT — À REMPLIR PAR L'ETUDIANT

1. SOCIAL INSURANCE NO OF CONTRIBUTOR / Nº D'ASSURANCE SOCIALE DU COTISANT
NAME OF CONTRIBUTOR — NOM DU COTISANT (Please print — Lettres moulées)

9 8 7 6 5 4 3 2 1

Mr / M, Miss / Mlle, Mrs / Mme, Ms / Md

Given name and initial — Prénom et initiale: GEORGE

Family Name — Nom de famille: GREEN

2. YOUR NAME — VOTRE NOM (Please print — lettres moulées) / YOUR SOCIAL INSURANCE NO / VOTRE Nº D'ASSURANCE SOCIALE

3 4 5 3 4 2 1 2 3

Mr / M, Mrs / Mme, Miss / Mlle, Ms / Md

Given name and initial — Prénom et initiale: SUE S.

Family Name — Nom de famille: GREEN

3. CHEQUE ADDRESS / ADRESSE D'ENVOI DU CHEQUE
(Number and Street — Numéro et rue): 305 Snort Street
(P.O. Box or R.R. No) — (C.P. ou nº R.R.):
(City, Town or Village) — (Ville ou village): Lethbridge
(Province or Territory) — (Province ou territoire): Alberta
(Country) — (Pays): Canada
(Postal Code) — (Code postal): ZIP CGC

4. HOME ADDRESS / ADRESSE DU DOMICILE IF DIFFERENT FROM CHEQUE ADDRESS / SI ELLE DIFFERE DE L'ADRESSE INDIQUEE CI-DESSUS
(Number and Street — Numéro et rue):
(P.O. Box or R.R. No) — (C.P. ou nº R.R.):
(Province or Territory) — (Province ou territoire):
(Country) — (Pays):
(Postal Code) — (Code postal):

5. ENROLLED AS A STUDENT AT / INSCRIT(E) COMME ELEVE A
Name of School, University, College, Junior College, Training Centre, etc — Nom de l'école, de l'université, du collège, du centre de formation, etc.) Lethbridge Agricultural College

6A. TYPE OF ENROLLMENT / SORTE D'INSCRIPTION
☒ FULL TIME / PLEIN TEMPS
☐ EVENING TIME / LE SOIR
☐ OTHER / AUTRE (Specify) Precisez
If "Evening" or "Other" please explain in 6 below / Si "Le soir" ou "Autre" veuillez expliquer au Nº 8 ci-dessous

6B. ENROLLED IN (Specify Course, Grade or Faculty) INSCRIT(E) (Précisez cours, grade ou faculté) Masters program in Agriculture

7A. NUMBER OF HOURS YOU ARE REQUIRED TO ATTEND PER WEEK FOR ABOVE COURSE, GRADE OF FACULTY NOMBRE D'HEURES DE PRÉSENCE REQUISES PAR SEMAINE, SELON LE COURS, LE GRADE OU LA FACULTÉ
Hours per week / Heures par semaine: 24

7B. WHEN DID OR WILL YOUR CURRENT ATTENDANCE BEGIN? QUAND VOTRE PRÉSENTE PÉRIODE DE COURS A-T-ELLE OU DOIT-ELLE COMMENCER?
Month / Mois: 09   Year / Année: 9-

7C. WHEN WILL YOUR CURRENT ATTENDANCE END? QUAND VOTRE PRÉSENTE PÉRIODE DE COURS DOIT-ELLE SE TERMINER?
Month / Mois: 04   Year / Année: 9-

8. REMARKS (Give duration and reasons for any absence(s) during your current and past academic year plus any additional explanation with reference to the question 6A above)
REMARQUES (Donner la durée et raison(s) pour toutes absences pendant votre année scolaire courante et precedente et ajouter tout detail additionnel par suite de la question 6A ci-dessus)   n/a

9. HAVE YOU APPLIED FOR OR ARE YOU RECEIVING A CPP BENEFIT AS A RESULT OF THE DISABILITY OR DEATH OF A CONTRIBUTOR NOT IDENTIFIED IN 1 ABOVE?
AVEZ-VOUS PRÉSENTE UNE DEMANDE OU RECEVEZ-VOUS UNE PRESTATION DU RPC SUITE A L'INVALIDITE OU LE DECES D'UN COTISANT NON IDENTIFIE AU Nº 1 CI-DESSUS?
☐ YES / OUI   ☒ NO / NON
SOCIAL INSURANCE NO OF THAT CONTRIBUTOR / Nº D'ASSURANCE SOCIALE DE CE COTISANT

I hereby declare that, to the best of my knowledge and belief, the information given above is true and complete. I UNDERTAKE TO NOTIFY THE CANADA PENSION PLAN ADMINISTRATION SHOULD I INTERRUPT OR TERMINATE MY ATTENDANCE AT SCHOOL OR UNIVERSITY. I hereby authorize the above school or university to provide the Canada Pension Plan Administration with information regarding my enrollment and attendance.
Par les présentes, je déclare que, a ma connaissance les renseignements contenus dans la présente déclaration sont vrais et complets. SI J'INTERROMPS MES COURS OU CESSE DE FREQUENTER L'ECOLE OU L'UNIVERSITE, JE M'ENGAGE A EN AVERTIR LA DIRECTION DU RÉGIME DE PENSIONS DU CANADA. En outre, j'autorise l'école ou l'université susmentionnée à donner à la Direction du Régime de pensions du Canada les renseignements relatifs à mon inscription et à ma frequentation.

DATE: June 20, 199-
SIGNATURE OF STUDENT — SIGNATURE DE L'ELEVE: Sue Green
TELEPHONE NO — Nº DE TELEPHONE: 123-4567

IT IS AN OFFENCE TO MAKE A FALSE OR MISLEADING STATEMENT IN THIS DECLARATION
C'EST UNE INFRACTION QUE DE FAIRE, DANS LA PRESENTE, UNE DECLARATION FAUSSE OU TROMPEUSE

SECTION B — TO BE COMPLETED BY SCHOOL OR UNIVERSITY — À REMPLIR PAR L'ECOLE OU L'UNIVERSITE
To the best of our knowledge and belief, the answers to the questions in Section A above, are correct unless otherwise stated below:
À notre connaissance, les réponses aux questions de la section A ci-dessus, sont exactes sous reserve de l'observation suivante:

Additional Comments — Commentaires additionnels:

NAME AND ADDRESS OF SCHOOL OR UNIVERSITY / NOM ET ADRESSE DE L'ECOLE OU DE L'UNIVERSITE

NAME OF AUTHORIZED PERSON — NOM D'UNE PERSONNE AUTORISEE

SIGNATURE

TITLE — TITRE

DATE

TELEPHONE NO / Nº DE TELEPHONE

FOR OFFICE USE ONLY / A L'USAGE EXCLUSIF DU BUREAU   CPP NO — Nº DE RPC

SAMPLE #30
APPLICATION FOR CHILD'S BENEFIT

Health and Welfare / Santé et Bien-être
Canada / Canada
Income Security / Programmes de la
Programs / sécurité du revenu

Français au verso
Personal Information
Bank NHW/P-PU-145
Bank NHW/P-PU-165

FOR PERTINENT INFORMATION WITH RESPECT
TO THE PRIVACY ACT, PLEASE SEE
INFORMATION SHEET

APPLICATION

CHILD'S BENEFIT

CANADA PENSION PLAN

— COMPLETE THE UNSHADED AREAS
— PLEASE PRINT

LANGUAGE PREFERENCE

ENGLISH ☒   FRENCH ☐

(BENEFIT FOR CHILD AGE 18 TO 25 AND IN FULL TIME ATTENDANCE AT SCHOOL OR UNIVERSITY)
THIS APPLICATION MUST BE SUPPORTED BY A DECLARATION OF ATTENDANCE AT SCHOOL OR UNIVERSITY FORM

SECTION A – INFORMATION ABOUT THE CONTRIBUTOR

1A. CONTRIBUTOR'S SOCIAL INSURANCE NUMBER: 9 8 7 6 5 4 3 1 1

1B. Male ☒ Female ☐

2. MR. MRS. ETC GIVEN NAME AND INITIAL: GEORGE   FAMILY NAME: GREEN

3. CONTRIBUTOR'S ADDRESS (Number and street): 1624 Long Street   (Apt. No. PO Box, R.R. No.)

4. (City, Town or Village): Calgary   (Province or Territory): Alberta   (Country): Canada   (Postal Code): 2 1 P 0 G 0

SECTION B – INFORMATION ABOUT THE CHILD OF THE CONTRIBUTOR

5A. CHILD'S SOCIAL INSURANCE NUMBER: 3 4 5 4 3 2 1 2 3

5B. Male ☐ Female ☒

6. MR., MRS. ETC GIVEN NAME AND INITIAL: SUE S.   FAMILY NAME: GREEN

7. HOME ADDRESS SAME AS IN 3 ABOVE ☐ OR (Number and street): 305 Short Street   (Apt. No. PO Box, R.R. No.)

8. (City, Town or Village): Lethbridge   (Province or Territory): Alberta   (Country): Canada   (Postal Code): 2 1 P 0 G 0

9. MAILING ADDRESS FOR CHEQUE IF DIFFERENT FROM 7 ABOVE (Number and street)   (Apt. No. PO Box, R.R. No.)

10. (City, Town or Village)   (Province or Territory)   (Country)   (Postal Code)

11A. ARE YOU DISABLED? ☐ Yes ☒ No

11B. DATE OF BIRTH: Day 2 5 Month 0 4 Year 7 -

AGE ESTABLISHED

12A. ARE OR WERE YOU EVER A BENEFICIARY OR AN APPLICANT FOR A BENEFIT UNDER
A. The Canada Pension Plan ☐ Yes ☒ No
B. The Quebec Pension Plan ☐ Yes ☒ No

12B. IF YES, INDICATE UNDER WHAT SOCIAL INSURANCE NUMBER

13. ARE YOU A NATURAL OR LEGALLY ADOPTED CHILD OF THE CONTRIBUTOR? ☒ Yes ☐ No
IF LEGALLY ADOPTED INDICATE DATE OF ADOPTION   Day   Month   Year

SECTION C – DECLARATION OF APPLICANT

14. I hereby apply for a Disabled Contributor's Child Benefit ☐   I hereby apply for an Orphan Benefit ☒

I declare that to the best of my knowledge and belief the information given in this application is true and complete and I undertake to notify the Income Security Programs Branch of any changes in the circumstances which may affect eligibility.

APPLICANT'S SIGNATURE: Sue S. Green
Date of Application: Day 3 0 Month 0 6 Year 9 -
Telephone Number: 654-3210

IT IS AN OFFENCE TO MAKE A FALSE OR MISLEADING STATEMENT IN THIS APPLICATION.

OFFICE USE ONLY — DO NOT WRITE BELOW THIS LINE

Application taken by   DATE APPLICATION RECEIVED

Application approved pursuant to Subsection 54(3) of the Canada Pension Plan   Date

Effective Date

Authorized Signature

127

GLOSSARY

ADMINISTRATOR
Individual appointed by the Surrogate Court to administer the estate of a person who dies without a will; feminine form — "administratrix"; or where no executor is named in the will; or where the executor named does not act

AFFIDAVIT
Statement sworn before a lawyer or notary public

BENEFICIARY
A person who derives some benefit, whether money or property, from the will of a deceased person or pursuant to the Intestate Succession Act

CAPITAL GAIN
Profit realized on the sale of an asset or the profit deemed to be realized as if the asset had been sold at the time of the owner's death

CAPITAL LOSS
Loss experienced on the sale of an asset or the loss deemed to be realized as if the asset had been sold at the time of the owner's death

CODICIL
An amendment to a will requiring all the formalities of execution needed for a will

CONSANGUINITY
The relation or connection of persons descended from the same ancestor

DEVISE
A disposition of land by will

ENCROACH
The act of paying out to the beneficiary portions of the money or other assets being held for that beneficiary in trust

THE FAMILY RELIEF ACT
The Alberta act that governs the right of dissatisfied dependants of the deceased to apply for a larger share of the estate

HOLOGRAPH WILL
A will written completely in the handwriting of the person making it, having no witnesses to the signature of the testator

INTESTATE
Either the act of dying without a will or the person who dies without a will

INTESTATE SUCCESSION ACT
The Alberta act governing the disposition of the property where the deceased left no valid will

ISSUE
All lineal descendants of the testator, i.e., children, grandchildren, etc.

LEGACY
Personal property or money given by a will. Also called a bequest

LIFE INTEREST
A benefit given to a beneficiary in a will that permits that beneficiary to enjoy or have the use of some property or some amount of money for the balance of the beneficiary's lifetime only

LETTERS OF ADMINISTRATION
The court grant appointing an administrator to administer the estate of an individual dying intestate

LETTERS OF ADMINISTRATION WITH WILL ANNEXED
The court grant appointing an administrator to administer the estate of an individual who left a will, where the named executor has died or is unable or unwilling to act

LETTERS PROBATE
The court grant confirming the appointment of an executor named in a will and confirming the validity of the will itself

NEXT-OF-KIN
Blood relatives of a person dying intestate who inherit by reason of the Intestate Succession Act

NOTARIAL COPY
True copy of an original document certified by a lawyer or notary public as being a true copy

PERSONAL PROPERTY
All property with the exception of real estate and buildings; also known as "personalty" (as opposed to "realty")

PERSONAL REPRESENTATIVE
The individual, either appointed in a will or appointed by the court, to administer and deal with the assets of an estate

PER STIRPES
A method of dividing assets of an estate such that if a member of the group among which the assets are being divided happened to be dead at the time of the division, the children of that deceased member of the group will divide among them the share that their parent would have received had he or she been alive

PROBATE
The process of "proving" a will

REAL PROPERTY
Land and buildings; also known as "real estate" or "realty"

RESIDUE
That portion of an estate remaining after all specific bequests and specific devices have been made

RESIDUARY BENEFICIARY
The beneficiary to whom the residue of the estate is left

SPECIFIC BEQUEST
A gift under a will of a specific item of personal property or a specific amount of cash

SPECIFIC DEVISE
A gift under a will of a specific item of real property

SURROGATE COURT
The court responsible for the appointment of personal representatives and generally involved with problems arising during the administration of estates. In Alberta it is a division of the Queen's Bench.

TENDENCIES
A man who makes a will; feminine form — "tendencies"

TRANSMISSION
Transfer of property to beneficiary after probate of will or letters of administration obtained

WILL
The legal statement of a person's wishes concerning the disposal of his or her property after death